Table of Contents

SQL Programming

The Ultimate Step-By-Step Guide to Learning SQL for Beginners

Python Programming
A Pragmatic Approach To Programming Python for Total Beginners

SQL Programming

The Ultimate Step-By-Step Guide to Learning SQL for Beginners

Introduction

Congratulations on purchasing *SQL Programming,* and thank you for doing so.

The following chapters will discuss everything that you need to know when you want to start implementing SQL and its databases into your business model. There is often a lot of information that a business needs to keep track of, from their customer information to their product information, and having an effective database to hold onto this information can make a big difference in the success that you will see. There are a few different databases that you can choose to work with, but the SQL language and database associated with it is becoming the industry standard overall.

There are a lot of different things that we are able to learn when it comes to the SQL language. To start, we are going to look at some of the basics that come with SQL. We will look at what this language is all about and why it has gained so much popularity in recent years. From there, we will move on to some of the basic commands that work with SQL, the different types of data that are recognized in this language, and some of the methods that you can use to manage this data.

Once we have spent some time handling the various objects that show up in these databases, we will talk about how to do a few of your own search results to find what you need and even how to work with relational database concepts. From there we will spend some time learning how to define some of the data that we want to use with the SQL language and can help us to make sure everything goes in the right place as we code.

The end of this guidebook is going to help us to explore a few important topics that come with using the SQL language. We will look at how to do a few important tasks like working with queries, views, and indexing, and then move on to keeping the database secure since it could potentially hold onto a lot of personal information, and your customers and other users expect you as a business to keep that information safe and away from the wrong hands. We will spend the last part of this book looking at some real-world situations when you can use the topics in this guidebook to get the results that you want with SQL.

2

As you can see, there are a lot of different options and topics that we need to explore when it comes to working with the SQL database and language. There may be other kinds of databases out there that you are able to work with, but none are going to work as well and provide you with the results that you want for your business. When you are ready to learn more about the SQL code and how to make it work, check out this guidebook to help you get started!

Books about the subject flood the market and we thank you for choosing this one! Please Enjoy!

Chapter 1: The Basics of SQL

If you are looking at learning one of the new coding languages that are available, you may notice that there are a lot of options out there that can be great to work with. Some of these are going to be designed with the beginner programmer in mind to make things easier. Some of these languages are going to be better to use with more advanced coders, work better with one kind of operating system over another, or will help with designing things like websites.

Another option that you can make when choosing a coding language to work with is SQL. This is a great coding language that can be used by businesses to make sure they stay properly organized and are able to keep track of customer and business information while avoiding some of the challenges that come with this as well.

Traditionally, it was common for many companies to work with what was known as the DBMS, or the Database Management System, to help them to keep this information organized, and to make sure they could keep track of their products and their customers. This was one of the very first options on the market for this kind of organization, and you will find that there are many things to enjoy about this system.

While DBMS is going to work well for helping you get some of the work done that you need to with databases, you will find that through the years, there are also a few newer methods that have been released that have changed the way companies will hold onto and sort their information. Even with some of the most basic systems for managing your data, you will see that there is more security and power in these versions than there was in the past.

Many larger companies are responsible for holding onto a lot of data, including some information that is personal about their customers. Information like names, address, and credit card information could be a goldmine if it isn't stored properly, and a hacker or someone else was able to get ahold of it. And as technology grows, it is important for businesses to be able to properly manage these systems and keep things in check and working well. Due to that the information that these companies need to hold is going to be more complex than ever before, the Relational Database Management System has been created in order to keep the information safe, much safer than the DBMS system was able to do in the past.

Now, if you are a business owner and need to keep track of valuable information about customers in your system, you will have a few choices in what you want to get out of a good database management system. While there are a few different options, the one that most companies will like to work with is the SQL. SQL language is one of the best options for doing this work, it is one of the easiest to work with, and was designed to work well with some businesses and will give you all of the tools that you need to make sure that all of your information is safe and sound.

There are a lot of reasons why you would want to protect the information of your customers. Not only will this help to keep your customers safe, but it ensures that your customers still have faith and trust in your business. The SQL language will be able to help you make sure this happens. Let us take a look at the SQL language and learn how to make this work well for your own business.

The SQL language is going to be unique compared to some of the other coding languages that you are able to use. It is going to work in a slightly different manner than some of the others. It is designed for you to be able to work with a database and create a lot of indices and tables that will work for your own needs.

Many companies are going to rely on these tables and databases to help them run. You can use them to help you keep your business employees in order and hold onto their information. You can have a database that helps to hold onto the work that each employee is doing and provides them with roles and access depending on the work that they do. You can even work with a database that helps you to keep track of customer information and some of the products that you are offering.

Let's look at a quick example. If you have a store that sells a variety of products, and you allow your customers to use a search box to type in the item that they want to look for, then you have worked with a database that may be working with SQL.

When the customer types in the term that they want to find, the SQL language is set up in a way that it is able to take that query and look through the database. If everything has been set up in the proper manner, then you will be able to get the right kinds of search results to show up in the next window. This helps the customer to find what they are looking for, without them having to go through your whole database to find the right product. This may not seem like a big deal if you have ten items for sale, but if you have 10,000 items, it can really make the process more efficient and the customer happier.

This is just one of the examples of what we are going to learn how to do with the SQL language. This language is so much easier than you may think it will be when you first get started. As we go through this guidebook, we will look at a few examples of the coding that you will need to do with this one, and you will be surprised at how easy it is and how much more you can do.

Microsoft®
SQL Serve

If you have ever worked with any other coding language in the past, or even taken a look at how they work, you may be a bit scared by all of the work and the complicated codes. But with SQL, you can use just one or two words on most of the codes, and then the database will do what you want. Let's dive into this and see a bit more about what you can do to see the results you want with your SQL database.

What is the SQL language?

The first thing to take a look at here before we do any coding is what the SQL language is all about. SQL is going to be a type of programming language that you can work with that stands for Structured Query Language. This language is pretty simple to learn because it helps you to interact with the different types of databases that you add to the same system. It also helps a company to keep track of the information that they have for their customers and for their products.

This database system first was released in the 1970s, but when IBM came out with its own type of programming language, we saw SQL really start to grow in popularity. It didn't take long before a lot of companies started to take notice and wanted to use this system.

The version of SQL that IBM was using went under the name of ORACLE. In fact, this became such a successful piece of technology that it wasn't long before there was a split and ORACLE left IBM and started out as its own company. ORACLE, due to some of the ways that it is able to work with SQL, is still one of the programming language leaders in the world, and it is easy to see some of the ways that this program is keeping up with changes in the database management and programming world.

ORACLE®

The SQL language is going to be like a set of instructions that you can use to help you have some interactions with your relational database. While there are going to be other coding languages that you can bring in to get this kind of work done, SQL is the only language that most databases used by companies will be able to understand.

This can make life easier when you already know how to use SQL and how to make it work for you. Any time that you want to interact with many of the databases out there, you will be able to use the SQL software to go in and translate any of the commands that you are given, whether you do this through some mouse clicks or with the use of form entries. These will then be turned over to SQL statements that the database is ready to interpret pretty easily.

As we go through this, you will find that this process has three main components, and we are going to discuss these in more depth later in this guidebook. But the three main ones that you will most likely work with include Data Definition Language, Data Control Language, and Data Manipulation Language.

If you have had a chance to work with other software programs that are driven by databases, then it is likely that some form of SQL has been used in it as well. It is likely that you were able to use the SQL program without even knowing that you were using it. For example, if you are working with a dynamic web page that has a database to drive, it will have forms inside. And if the forms are filled out and clicked on to get to the database, then the information is composed into an SQL query. The query is then able to go through and get the information, or store the information, with the database and do the action that is needed.

Let us take a look at how this is going to work. If you are on a website looking through an online catalog for something, you will want to keep on searching until you find an item that you want. The search page that you use will often contain a form with a simple text box. If you don't want to go through and look at every page for that catalog, you will need to type in the search query, and it will take a look at and bring up the results.

The SQL in this part is going to use the information that you typed in and look through the database to see what it can find that matches up with the search term that you used. As soon as you do click on the search button, the webserver, with the help of SQL, will be able to go through and see if the database will find anything related to that search term. It can then bring back the items that match on a new web page and hopefully, if it is working well and the items have been stored in the proper manner, you will be able to find the things that you want through the database.

For those who haven't been able to work with a learning programming language, and who haven't done any coding, you may find that the commands that are needed to make the SQL language work will not be that hard. Commands that are present in SQL are all designed with a syntax that fits in with the English language.

You will be able to start with a command statement that you will use to describe the action you wish the program to take. From there you will have a clause that follows this and that helps describe the target of the command. This could include something like a specific table in the database that is affected by the command. And to finish this off, there is going to be a series of clauses that are responsible for providing the information that is needed.

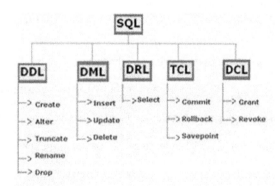

While this may seem like a lot of steps to keep track of for a beginner, it is just a few steps, and then you will have a command done that tells the database what you need to pull out. Often you may find that just by reading out the SQL statement, it is going to help you to figure out what you can get the command to do. A good example of how the code can work is below:

DELETE

FROM students

WHERE graduation_year = 2014

Read out the code above, and you can get a good idea of what is going to happen when you decide to execute it. Most of the codes that are presented in this program are going to work in a similar manner to this, which means it is easy for us to figure out how to write the codes that you would like. It won't take long to be able to read through the codes, make sure that everything is in place, and to do the actions that you would like.

If you have never been able to work with any kind of programming language in the past, then you will likely feel a bit worried about working with this and how to get it all set up for yourself. But we are going to explore a bit more about what you can do with this language, and the control that you can use over any database that relies on SQL as well.

Using SQL to work with your database

If you do decide that the SQL language is the right one for you to use when it is time to manage your database, then we need to go back through and look at the database a bit. As you are looking at this notice how the database is just going to contain groups of information. Some people may call these a kind of organizational mechanism that is used to store information that you can go back and look at later on. It can do this as effectively as possible. And SQL will make sure that you have all of the tools that you need to effectively manage any database that you want.

There are going to be some times when you work with some kind of project, and you are working on a database that shares many similarities to SQL. And you may have already been doing this in the past without realizing what was going on. For example, one database that you may have used at some point is a phone book. It may not be the traditional database that we consider, but you will find that it includes the name of a person, their address, their phone number, and even their business if you are in the yellow pages. And all of it is in one place like databases are supposed to be making it easier to find the information that you want quickly and effectively.

This is similar to the way that an SQL database is going to work as well. This language can find the information that you want by looking through the information that is available on any database that you give to it. It can then sort through that information so that you have the best chance of finding the information that you want, without a bunch of searchers and without adding in a lot of time in the process.

Relationship databases

With that in mind, we need to jump in and look at some of the different things that you can do with databases and SQL, and some of the other information that is going to help us get a good start. First, we need to look at the relational database. This is the database that you will work with when you have a database that is aggregated into tables or logical units, and then you want to be able to have the ability to connect the inside of your database, in a manner that makes the most sense for what is asked for at that time.

This is a lot to think of at this time. This kind of database is going to be a good option to use if you would like to take a look at information that is complex. Then, when that information has been looked over, you want to get the program to break down the information into some smaller pieces so that it is easier for you to manage the whole thing.

There are different times when you will want to work with the relational database. This is because they will allow you to take up all of the information that a particular business has stored, and then you can manipulate the information in a way that makes it easier to use, and even easier to read through and learn about in the long run.

You can use the relational database to take some of the complex information that you have available, and then break that up into smaller pieces where others can see what is going on and what is going to work the best for you. To make this a bit easier, this kind of system can go through a database and all of the information inside of it and then will make sure that the information is sorted and ready to go in no time at all.

It is also possible to go through this process and add in a bit more security. Meaning that if you do need to add in some customer personal information at one point, it will ensure that this information is kept as safe as possible, especially when it comes to those who would want to take the information and use it for their own personal gain.

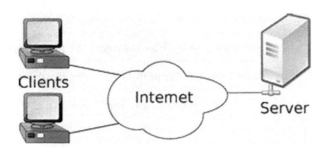

The client and server technology

In the past, if you were trying to do some computer work for your business, you were likely working with a mainframe computer. What this means is that the machine you were using would hold onto the large system, and then this system would be the part that would store all of the information that was needed to do the processing.

The user would be able to get onto the computer when needed and interact back with the mainframe, which would be known as a dumb terminal because it is not able to interact all on its own.

Now, if it were true that the user wanted to be able to get the information to show up with the correct function that they need, then the terminal would need to be able to rely on the information that is found inside of the computer, including the storage, the processor, and the memory.

At this point, you may see that the traditional manner may work well, and wonder why we would need to change anything up at all. They were able to get the job done for a company for a long time which made them very popular and, likely, some companies would not want to change it out at all. If you are already using this kind of system and you don't want to pay to get an upgrade, then it is going to do the work good enough. But with the help of SQL, there are a lot of options out there that are more popular and easier to use, and these are going to be found with a system known as the client-server system.

When we are looking at the client-server system, you will see that the system is going to use a different process to get the results that you would like. The main computer in this one is going to be known as the server, and it is technically available to anyone who is considered on the network.

Not just anyone can get on the server though. The user who tries needs to have the right kind of credentials before they are allowed because this adds to a level of security and safety to the process. But if the user comes to the network with the right information, and is found to be a part of the network, they will be able to gather the right information that they need in no time.

The user can get to the server from any other computer that they are using, and in this case, they will be known as the client for this process. This helps to make sure that both the client and the server, or the user and the main computer, can interact with each other with the help of this kind of database to get it done.

Working with the online database

As a business owner, you may find that the client and server technology that we just talked about is going to be the one that works the best for you. This system is great in many cases, but there are going to be some things that you will have to take away or add at times because of all the changes that have been happening to it later. Because of this, some companies are moving their databases online because this opens up some freedom and ensures that the database is going to work with any client, no matter where that client is located.

If you have ever signed up for an account with a company and had to come up with your own username and password, then you have likely worked with one of these databases in the past. As the trend continues for more companies to move their work online, it is going to be more common, and many of the databases that are in use today are going to be moved online as well.

Before a company decides to do this though, it is important for them to take the time to add in some extra security, especially when compared to some of the databases that they may have used in the past. There are hackers and others with ill-intentions who would love to collect the valuable information from places like Amazon, and security is of utmost importance to protect the customers if you do decide to move the database online.

Some of the reasons that SQL is so beneficial!

Now that we have a better idea when it comes to what SQL is all about and why some companies are going to want to use this to work with their own databases, it is time to look a bit more at some of the benefits that come with this language. There may be some other database languages that help you do the same thing, and there are certainly a lot of programming languages that can be adapted to do the work as well. Why is SQL so special, and why would you want to use it for your own needs?

There are several benefits that come with using the SQL language to deal with some of the databases that you have, and some of the best benefits are going to include:

1. Incredibly fast: If you would like to work with a type of management system that can work with the information quickly, and it is possible to get the results back that you need in no time, then the SQL language is a great option to go with. It only takes a few searches using this language to see just how responsive and quick it can be.

2. Standards that are well defined. The database that works with the SQL language is one that has been working well for a long period of time. It also has some great standards that will make sure the database is strong and will work out the way that you would like. There may be other databases out there that are similar, but their standards are lower, and this can make your work a bit frustrating.

3. There isn't a ton of coding. Yes, SQL is known as a programming language. But you don't have to learn lines and lines of coding in order to make this work. As we go through this guidebook, you will notice that there are a lot of codes we practice, and they don't require a ton of work either.

4. Keeps the database organized. When you are trying to run your business, it is important that you can keep the information secure and safe, as much as possible. And while other databases strive to do this, they are not going to help you get all of this security done like SQL can for you.

5. Object-oriented DBMS: The database that comes with SQL is going to rely on the DBMS system that we talked about earlier. The reason that it does this is that this all makes it easier to find any of the information that you need, stores the right items at the right time, and can make it easier to do the other actions that you need in this database.

Above is just a few of the different benefits that you can get when you decide to work with this language. While some people find that the interface of SQL is going to be different than what they have worked with in the past, it is something easy to work with, and before long, you will find that if you are working with a database of any kind, then the SQL language is the best one to get started with.

Chapter 2: Basic Commands That Work Well in SQL

Now that we have had a bit of time to learn more about the SQL language and how this kind of language works, along with some information about databases and how SQL works with these databases, it is time to get to work! Now we are going to look a bit more at the SQL system and look at some of the different commands that you will need to use to make sure the SQL system is going to do the exact actions and searches that you would like.

While it may sound like we are just jumping right into this and can seem a bit scary, don't worry. SQL is one of the easiest languages for you to learn how to use, and the codes are some of the easiest to write out of all the other coding languages. This will ensure that those who are beginners can work with this language as well.

To help us out with some of the commands that you need to learn how to use in SQL, we are going to need to split each of them into six different categories. Each of these categories is important to do some of the code that we want, but doing this will make it easier to understand how each one works with the others and with the program. The six categories of SQL language that you can work with includes:

<u>Data definition language</u>

The first category that we need to take a look at is going to be known as the data definition language or DDL<. It is one of the aspects that are in charge of allowing you to generate some new items into a pre-existing database before you go through and arrange these new objects in the way that makes the most sense for your needs.

For example, this is going to be the part of this system that you will want to use any time that you need to make any change to the table of your database. So, if you want to add in a new object or delete an object, the DDL is going to help. There are a few different commands that are going to fit into this category and they include:

1. Drop index

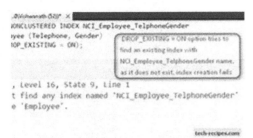

2. Alter an index

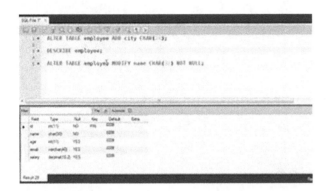

3. Drop view

4. Create an index

5. Alter a table

6. Drop a table

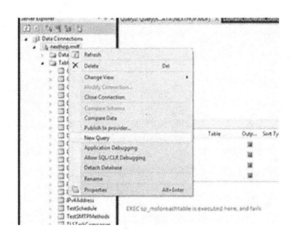

7. Create a table

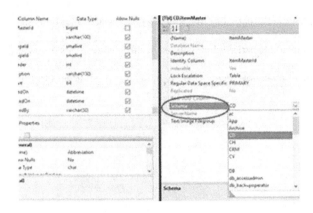

Data manipulation language

The second category that we can put our commands into will be the data manipulation language or the DML. This is going to be the part of the system that you are able to use when you would like to take some of the objects that are in your database and then try to modify them. This is going to make it easier because you and the user have some freedom when doing a search of the information found in the database, and can sometimes free up some more room so that you can add in information that is newer or more relevant at that time.

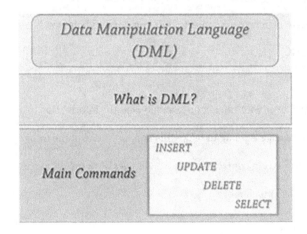

Data control language

On to the next category for your commands in SQL. This is the category that you are going to use any time that you need to add in a bit of power to the codes that you decide to write when you are writing codes. This one will work the best when you want to have a bit more control over how many people, or who can get access to the database that you have made.

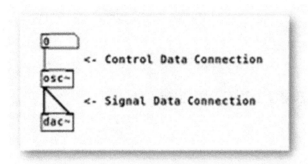

If your company is making a database that may have a lot of personal information about the customer, including their names, their address and their credit card information, it is best if you can work with this data control language. This is going to give you the ability to place limits on who can use the database and who can access the information. Some of the things to remember when you decide to work with the data control language include that the DCL command is going to be used to help generate any objects that you need to help you have control over who accesses the information in the database.

There are times when you need to have a bit of control over who can get onto and look at the information in a database, and who has to be kept out. The data control language is going to make this happen. Some of the things that you are able to do with this kind of command will be getting control over those who get onto the database, who can distribute any of the information that is on it, and so much more.

There are a few different commands that you are able to work with when it comes to the data control language commands, and some of these include:

1. Create synonym
2. Grand
3. Alter password

4.   Revoke

Data administration commands

As you work with some of the different commands that show up in the system, you will also find that there are some that are able to audit and analyze the operation that is found in the database. There may also be times where you would like to access how the database is performing with the database overall, as long as you use the right commands to make it happen.

If you are working on one of your databases, and you would like to be able to fix something that is not necessarily working the way that you would like inside of the database, or you feel that there are a few bugs in the system that you want to be able to take care of and remove from the system, then the data administration commands are going to help to make this happens. Some of the commands that you are able to use that fit into this include:

1.   Start audit
2.   Stop audit

One of the things that we have to remember when we use this, and when we are working with the SQL system is that the data administrator and the database administrator are going to be two different things. So, the database administrator is going to be the person in the coding that is able to manage all the aspects that come with the database, including some of the commands, and has the total control for doing this.

Transactional control commands

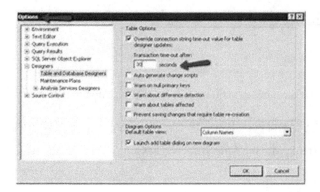

There are going to be times when you will need to manage, as well as keep track of, a lot of transactions that happen in the database. If you are trying to do some of these actions in the database, you will need to work with what is known as the transactional control commands to make this work. If you are a company that plans to use their own website to help sell some products, then the transactional control commands are going to help make sure everything stays organized. There are a few things that you are able to use this kind of command for including the following:

1. Commit: This is going to be the type of command that you will use when you would like to save some information that relates to the various transactions that show up in the database.

2. Savepoint: this is another command that you will use when it is time to generate two or more points in a group of transactions. You can also use it along with the rollback command to get more done.

3. Rollback: This is the command that you are able to use when it is time to take a look through your database, and you are trying to see which thing you are able to undo inside of your database.

4. Set transactions: With this command, you will be able to use it any time that you would like to provide a name to the transactions that you can find in the database. The set transaction is going to make it easier to label the things that you would like to end up with more organization in the system overall.

As you can see here, there are a lot of different things that you are able to do when it comes to the commands in the SQL language. They are going to make sure that you get the most possible out of the searches and can help the database to provide you with any information that is needed. We will look at some more about these codes

23

and these commands as we go through, but having some basics down and understanding how the system works can make a big difference in the kind of results that you will see.

Chapter 3: Are There Different Types of Data to Use in SQL?

Now that we have had some time to look at the different commands that come with SQL, it is time to take a look at some of the data types that need to come with the process as well when you are creating new code. These types of data are going to change on occasion, based on the action that you would like to complete on your own inside the database. It can also depend on the products that you want to offer to and even sell to the customers.

	postgresql	sqlite	sqlserver	sybase
:binary	bytea	blob	image	image
:boolean	boolean	boolean	bit	bit
:date	date	date	date	datetime
:datetime	timestamp	datetime	datetime	datetime
:decimal	decimal	decimal	decimal	decimal
:float	float	float	float(8)	float(8)
:integer	integer	integer	int	int
:string	(note 1)	varchar(255)	varchar(255)	varchar(255)
:text	text	text	text	text
:time	time	datetime	time	time
:timestamp	timestamp	datetime	datetime	timestamp

The different types of data that you are likely to find in this kind of system will be the attributes that can go with the information that is on the inside, and then you can use these characteristics to get things placed on the table. When the characteristics are in the table, you are able to read them, fix them, modify them, and retrieve them any time that you need.

To help us get a better understanding of how this is going to work and why the SQL data types are important here, we need to look at an example. You are working on a program or a database, and you want to make sure that one particular field is going to be able to hold nothing except numeric values. You can use the SQL system to set this up to ensure that if the user tries to put in letters, that the table will make an error or they are not able to type up anything at all and they can just type in numbers. This could be done when you want the person to just write in their phone number, their credit card number, or their zip code.

With this idea, if you have a cell on your database table that needs to just have numbers on it, such as the phone number, then you would need to add in this kind of restriction to the code. By assigning the right data types to the fields that are going to show up in the table, you can solve some problems ahead of time and can make sure that the customer will see fewer errors in the long term.

One thing that we need to remember with this one is that when you work with this system, all of the versions are going to be slightly different, and the way that you do this process, and some of the choices that you are able to make with it are going to change up as well. You need to check out the rules that come with the SQL version that you plan to work with to make sure that it is going to work the way that you would like.

To help us work with the types of data in this system, it is important for you to know the basic types ahead of time. No matter which version of SQL you are working with, there are going to be three types of data that show up in each part, and these include:

1. Character strings
2. Tie and date values
3. Numeric strings

The character strings

The first thing that we are going to take a look at when it comes to data types in SQL is the character strings. We need to take a look at the fixed-length characters first. If you plan to work with some constant characters or even some strings that you want to make sure stay the same all of the time, you have to take the right steps, and use the right restrictions, to make sure that they get saved inside of your system in the right manner. The data type that is going to work the best for this to ensure that you pick out characters in the proper manner includes the following sample:

CHARACTER (n)

Take a look at the example below, and notice that there is an 'n' that we are able to place in the code above. This one is going to be important because it is going to be the assigned length, and sometimes the maximum length, that you are going to allow to show up in a particular field.

Let's say that you choose to use this as a phone number field. You would want to set the n at 10 because that is as many numbers as you want to allow inside of that part of the table. This is just one example of how you could work with when it comes to limiting your characters. This works fine if you want to have the user put in the phone number or zip code, for example. But if you put this into something like the name part, you will end up cutting some people out of the mix because their name is longer than the maximum that you had put into the code.

Depending on what kind of version that you have with SQL, you can find that you will need to work with the CHAR data type rather than the CHARACTER that we did before to set up the fixed-length that you are going to work with. It is often a good idea for you to work with this data type if you want the information that the user adds in to be alphanumeric.

So with this one, you would end up placing the name of their state, but you want to make sure that they are using the abbreviation, such as NE rather than Nebraska, rather than the whole name of the state in this process. You would be able to use the character limit to just two here so that the other person can figure out what they need to do here.

When the data type of character comes up, your user is not going to add in information that is longer than the character limit you set. If the phone number is needed, you will need to set it at ten. If you want to limit the length of the state, you would put it at two characters. It will all be dependent on the kind of forms that you want to use, and the information that is going to become a part of your set of data as you do things.

The variable characters

Now that we have a good idea what the character strings are going to be, it is time to move on to the second thing that you can fix here. This is going to be the variable characters. It is possible that you are able to work with the variable characters rather than the fixed length characters that we had in the last sections. Rather than only allowing the user to go with so many characters, you can also ask the user to pick out how long this whole thing should be.

This is something that you will want to do in situations like when the user needs to write out their name, including the usernames and the passwords, and more. This allows the user to put in their full name, and then they get the choice of making the username and their password as unique as they will need. To make this notation work in the SQL code, you will need to use the following code to help.

CHARACTER VARYING (n)

Using the code that we have above, you are going to see that the n is going to be the number that you are able to use in order to identify the maximum or the assigned value. You will then need to go through and pick out a form there more than one kind of option that you would like to put in there to help with the characters. Some of the options that you are able to choose here in terms of the variable characters include ANSI, VARCHAR, and VARCHAR2.

For the type of data that we are working with here, there is not going to be any requirement that you have to meet for filling out space. The user is not going to be limited here, which can be nice in many situations. If you did go through and add in a limit of 15 characters, this one would allow the user to write out an answer that is anywhere up to 15 characters. They could also do less than 15 if that is what they want, and it would go through as well.

Any time that you would like to do a few character strings that are going to be more variable, such as a name rather than something like a state abbreviation, you will want to work with the various characters. The reason for working on this is because it allows for us to maximize the space that you are able to use in your database and it can help the user to put in the information in the correct manner, without any errors or confusion showing up in the database in the process.

Numeric value

In addition to working with the two options for characters that we talked about before in terms of the length of the variables that you do, you will also be able to work with the numeric values and how you are able to use it in the SQL language. It is possible to add in values that are numeric at any point that it makes sense with your code. You won't want to add in numbers during the name point of course, but in other options, you will be able to do it for other parts as needed in the code.

These values are going to be the ones that you are able to store right in the field with the use of a number, without needing to add a character if the user doesn't want to. These values are going to come in with a few different names based on which numeric value you would like to use in the code. However, there are some that are more common to work with, and the options that you can include in your code includes:

1. Decimal
2. Real
3. Bit
4. Float
5. Integer
6. Double precision
7. Bit varying(n)

Literal strings

The next option that we need to take a look at here is going to be the literal strings. These are going to consist of a series of characters, and the length of these will be as long or as short as you need. It could be the name and the phone number that will be specified by either the database or the user based on what you are trying to do at the time. For the most part, these strings will be able to hold onto a ton of data, as long as the data held into it is going to be characteristics that go with it.

Now, if you do decide to work with some of these literal strings, you may find that you can run into trouble when it is time to specify the data type you would like to work with. When this happens, you may need to spend some time specifying the type of string that you want to use so that you can double-check that it is going to work the way that you would like. It is good to understand that when you do this, especially if you are working on a string that includes letters and numbers, you need to have some quotes that go around the world to make it work better. You can pick either to use double or single quotes, as long as you use them the same on both sides.

Working with the Boolean values

In many cases, you are going to get into the Boolean values when you work in SQL because they help you do many functions in this system, and they will make it easier to complete the searchers that you or your user will want to do in the database. There are three options that come with the Boolean values, and we are going to take a look at each of them. The three options that come with the Boolean values are going to include true, false, and null.

p	q	p OR q	p AND q	p = q
True	True	True	True	True
True	False	True	False	False
True	Unknown	True	Unknown	Unknown
False	True	True	False	False
False	False	False	False	True
False	Unknown	Unknown	False	Unknown
Unknown	True	True	Unknown	Unknown
Unknown	False	Unknown	False	Unknown
Unknown	Unknown	Unknown	Unknown	Unknown

p	NOT
True	False
False	True
Unknown	Unknown

As you write out some codes that have Boolean values, you may find that using these will be helpful when you are trying to compare more than one data in the table at the same time. You would be able to use these units together with the Boolean value to compare whether the two or more parts are the same or not. This is a good way to set up some of the parameters that come with the search, and when things are compared together and seen as similar, then those would be the results that show up for you.

With the Boolean values, it is important to remember that it is only going to give you some results when an answer comes back as true. If the answer to these values is either false or null, the data is not going to be taken out of the database at this time. If the answer is going to be true, then this is what will show up on the screen when you are done with the query.

A good way to explore this a bit more is when the user is trying to utilize the database and you are trying to find something that is inside a large amount of information. If you are searching for a product, for example, the

30

Boolean values would be able to help you here. If the keywords of the product match up with the query that you are doing, then the ones that match will come up on the screen, and the others will not join the list.

If you are a business with your own website and you are trying to sell a few things online, you may find that it is common for you to use these Boolean values, which is why we are spending some time exploring this topic now. These values are going to be responsible for making sure that when a query is done on your website by a user, the right results that match up with that query will show up on the computer.

There are going to be a lot of different applications where you are able to use the Boolean expressions inside of this language, but as someone who is just learning how to work with this language, this is probably the way that you would use the Boolean expressions the most. You can also use it any time that you have your own personal database, and you can find some answers to a question that you have, or when you are looking through the store or program, and you are trying to get things to match up.

Whether you are looking for using these Boolean values to help you to create a website that finds the results that someone is looking for when they search through your products, or you are using it to go through your own database to find the information that you need, the Boolean values are going to be there to help you get this done. They work on the idea of the answers being true, false or null, so if the products are set up in the database in the proper manner, you will find that you should get the right products to match up with the queries users submit when you use the idea of the Boolean expressions.

As you can see with the different topics we have discussed in this chapter, there are a lot of different types of data that you are able to work with when you choose the SQL language. Using these different types of data in the right place will help to make searches easier, and will ensure that your program is going to work the right way each time.

Chapter 4: Managing Objects in SQL

This guidebook has taken a bit of time for us to look over the different topics and the types of data that is important for this kind of language, it is time to take a look at some of the methods that you are able to use to help manage objects. There are a lot of different techniques that you are able to use when it comes to managing some of your objects in SQL, so let's get started!

Looking at the schema

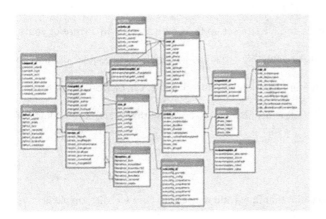

The first topic that we are going to talk about in this chapter is known as a schema. With these schema's, you will think of it as using a set of objects that you can already find in the database, but which need to be linked back to one user, rather than to all of the users, who are on that database. This means that just one user is going to be able to access the schema and see the objects that are inside of it.

Think of this like having your own account on a website. The user may be able to use some of their personal information like address, username, credit card information, and more, along with some of their purchases in the past. This is information that only the user would be able to access with the use of their username and password, and other users on that same database, unless they had this information, would not be able to access the account.

The objects that are on that part of the database, or for the account, are going to be linked directly back to whatever username the owner decided to pick out. The user will then have the power to generate objects, and when this is all done, it is time for them to finish the process to generate a brand new schema. This is a neat thing because it ensures that the user is able to control what is found in their own personal database, and they can make the changes to that database that they see fit.

You will find that there are several ways that this is going to be helpful. In one instance, the user may be in need of placing an order with a company. If the user already has their own account, which would consist of their own schema, they would be able to make and place the order, and then they would be able to delete or change the order if they choose. They can even go through and delete an order or change it when they need to.

Often this is going to be shown when the user goes and tries to set up their own account in a store of yours. This is something that they can optionally decide to do or something that you as the business require them to do in order to make the purchase. This allows them to have an account in the store and they can pick out the password and the username that they want to have associated back with the account, ensuring that there is some level of security that goes with it.

Once your new user has been able to set up the account that they want to use with your website, they will have access to any of the database that actually pertains to them. They can look up their orders, and what they have saved, they can look at the items and products for sale and more. But they will be a bit restricted because, for example, they will not be able to take a look at things like what orders another customer, in particular, has placed.

Now it is time to take a closer look at how this is going to work through an example. You want to set up some credentials for any user who wants to get onto the database, the credentials that they have to meet in order actually to use the sight. If they don't have the right credentials, then the security you set up will make sure they are not allowed on the system at all.

For this example, we are going to make our own username be PERSON1. You can then decide what information can be inside of the PERSON1 database, and you can even start up your own table that is just going to work with this username, maybe we will call it EMPLOYEES_TBL to make it easier. To see a bit more about how this works, when you decide to go into the records, you will notice that with this table, it is going to be labeled as PERSON1

EMPLOYEES_TBL. This is how others are going to see the name of the table as well because it helps them to know who is responsible for creating the table. The schema here is going to be the same, but it will include the username that was chosen, and then the name of the table that they pick as well.

When anyone is trying to access the schema that belongs to them, you will not need to list out the exact name of the schema that they are in. you would just need to pull up the name that was given to the table. So, for the example that we took some time on before, you would just need to pull up EMPLOYEES_TBL. The schema already knows what your username is, and it knows that you do not have access to the other tables, so the PERSON1 is not necessary with this.

Creating a new table

When it comes to working with databases, it is important to create lots of tables, ones that make sense and can store information for you in a neat and orderly fashion. There are a lot of different tables that you are able to use with the SQL language, so having a good understanding of them will make it easier. And the first thing that we are going to do in order to work with these tables and make sure that they can hold onto the information that you want is to create our first table.

Any time that you would like to create your own table in the SQL language, you will just need to use the command CREATE TABLE. It is as simple as that (remember we said SQL was easy to learn and write out!). This is the command that you can use to bring up the table and start using it, but we do need to take a few more steps before you are able to fill it in with the information that you need. This simply makes sure that we get the framework of the table set up so that it is ready for the writing later.

Before you use this command though, you have to stop and think about the way that you would like to have the table look, the kind of information that you plan to add to the table, how bit the table needs to be, along with any other information that may influence the final product of your table. Don't worry though, no matter which version of the SQL language you decide to work with, there will be options here that help you to create the table you want, even if you have no experience with this at all.

Creating a table based on one that already exists

The next thing that we need to look at is how you would be able to create a brand new table that is based on the information that you would be able to find in another table that was already written. There will be some times with this language where you have some information from an older table that you would like to keep and use for information to make a new one. This can save you a lot of time when you need to reorganize the information that you have and when you want to make sure the table comes out looking nice in the end.

The commands that you will need to do with this one will start out with CREATE TABLE as we used before, and then you will also need the command of SELECT. Once you have been able to work with both of these commands, you will see that it is responsible for creating a new table, one that has the same definitions and parameters as the old table you are copying from.

This can be a great feature that makes your database creation easier and will save you some time as well as potential mistakes. This is a good one that can help you to create a brand new table that you can then change up and customize the way that you want, while still using the information that you need from the older table.

Since we are looking at a coding language here, there is going to be a little bit of coding that we have to focus on to make sure that this new table is created, and that it is going to contain the information that you need from the original table. If you want to use the old table as the basis for a new table, then the syntax that you need to use to make this happen includes:

```
CREATE TABLE NEW_TABLE_NAME AS
SELECT [*/COLUMN1, COLUMN2]
FROM TABLE NAME
[WHERE];
```

As you look back at the syntax that we have above, you should be able to see that the two parts that we talked about above, the fact that you need the CREATE TABLE and the SELECT commands, were used in this, so we know that we did most of it right (or at least this part). The SELECT keyword is perfect to use here because it is the

36

command that you are able to use any time that you are working on a query for a particular database. This keyword is going to work to make sure that the new table will be created the way that you want, using the search results to get this done.

How to drop the tables you don't want

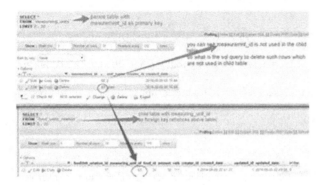

One final topic that we need to take a look at here when we work on the SQL language is how we are able to go through and drop tables. If you are able to use a brand new keyword that we are going to introduce now the RESTRICT keyword, and then you reference the table that you want by using the constraint or the view that you set up, you will be well on your way. Often you are going to see the keyword DROP used with this one too, but this can often give you more of an error signal in your system.

Another option that you can try to use with this kind of code, in addition to using the two above, would be the CASCADE command that shows up along with your DROP command. This has to happen to make sure that the DROP command is going to work in the right way and that all of the constraints and the views that are already found inside of the table you are working on will actually be dropped. An example of a code that you are able to use to make all of this happen will be below:

DROP TABLE TABLE_NAME [RESTRICT | CASCADE]

Any time that you would like to go through your database and drop a new table inside of it, you need to make sure that the program has a good idea who the owner of that table is. Sometimes the program will take the information without this part, but it is a good habit to get into because it helps to keep the database organized and will make sure that everyone has an idea of who is in charge of that new table.

Adding the name of the person who owns the table is going to help with a lot of issues including making sure that you don't lose the information or that you don't accidentally drop the wrong table in the process. If you have access to not only your own table but to other accounts as well, naming the tables properly will make sure that you don't get confused and that you are able to find the information that you need easily.

Since you will end up working with a ton of information when you do a database with SQL, it makes sense that these tables are an important part of making this kind of system work the way that you would like. The tables are going to help you not only to gather up the information that is important at that time, but they are going to present it and lay everything out in a way that is easiest to read.

From there, the tables that you create will be able to take the information, or perhaps the products that you would like to sell, and they can present them to you in a way that is easier for you and for other users to look through. Or you are able to set up the table so that the user when they are visiting the website and their own accounts, will be able to see the information laid out well.

Creating the tables in the SQL language is not supposed to be something that is difficult. We did several codes in this chapter that show us exactly how we would be able to set these up, without having to worry about it being too difficult or even worrying about how difficult it is to read the code. Creating these tables is one of the best ways to organize the information that you want to keep in your database and can make it easier to draw it out and use it at any time that you would like.

Chapter 5: Doing Your Own Search Results

We have mentioned a few times through this guidebook how people are able to get on the database for SQL and then do some search queries, you are able to do this a lot with this kind of language because it ensures that you are able to find the information that you want out of the database, without having to read every single item. You don't really want to go through and try to read through all of the items that Amazon has for sale. This is millions of products, and it could take forever before you find the product that you want. Doing a search query with the help of the SQL language will help you to get through this and find the results that actually match up what you need.

The SQL language is set up to work with searches and can be a great way for you and other users of the database to search for items and terms and make sure that the things that actually match up with that are going to show up on the screen. This is one of the fastest and most effective ways that you are able to sort through the information that you find in the database so that you make sure it is organized in the right way and to ensure that the right items that match your results show up on the screen as well here.

Once you have been able to go through the process of creating your own database or website for your business, and you have gone through the last chapter to make sure you know how to create and design the tables that you need, it is time to look through how to make your own queries and get accurate results with this system.

You have the benefit here because you are able to make the SQL language work for you to ensure that you are able to find any result that you want, as long as that information is found inside your database. Before you go through and do this though, you have to make sure that any database you plan to use is set up in the right manner so that any time you do one of these queries, the right information is going to show up without any problems.

One of the best ways for you to think about this process is that at times, someone is going to come and check out your website because they want to find a particular type of product that you have available. In this case, are you more interested in providing them with a database that is slow or will give those results that are not accurate? This may turn out to be the least expensive method in many cases, but it is just going to result in the user getting angry and frustrated. And with all of the competition that is out there, it is also likely that the user is going just to find another company to purchase from, and you will lose out on a sale.

A better option is to make sure that the database is set up in the proper manner so that it works quickly, and it will provide the user with the results that they are looking at. And that is what we are going to focus on inside of this chapter. Our job here is to learn some of the best codes and practices that you can use in order to set up the queries that you are using and get them to work well in the database while providing the best results for you.

How to create your own query

So, the first place to start here is to look at the best way to create a query in the SQL language. Before you start writing out your queries, just remember that when you send out this query, you are sending out information so that it reaches to a database that you set up previously. You want to make sure that the right command, which is the SELECT command, is the part used in this query, no matter what you plan to lookup.

Let's take a look at an example of how this is going to work. You may be working with one table, and the responsibility of that table is to hold onto the products that you listed out in the database. To help you get this done, you would need to use the SELECT command, and then the products are all going to be listed out for you. Of course, it is likely that the user is going to want a specific product that you are selling, so then they would need to type in the product they want, along with some of the other specifications they want, such as a price point and more, and then submit. If the database is set up in the proper manner, they will end up getting the results that they want.

Understanding the SELECT command a bit more

We have already spent a bit of time talking about the importance of the SELECT command and how this is going to make sure that we are able to read through the database that we have. Anytime that you are trying to work with the website, or you need to go into the database and create a new query, you will need to bring out that SELECT command to make it all happen. This command is really versatile, and it is going to take over the task of starting and executing any queries that you plan to send out to the databases.

To make this easy, you need to work with the SELECT command and then add in something to the statement to tell the database exactly what you are looking for. Sending out just the SELECT command will not tell the database what you want. You are able to add in any kind of search time that you would like after the command, but make sure it is there to help the command know where to search in the database.

Any time that you want to bring out this kind of command in the SQL language, there are going to be four main keywords that are important and will be a part of this process as well. We are going to take a look at these. Keep in mind that these four keywords are going to be referred back to as the four clauses so if you hear them by that name, we are talking about the same thing. The four clauses that you may encounter as you work with this command include:

SELECT

This is the command that you can use as long as it is combined with the command FROM. When these two keywords are put together, they are going to make sure that you have the right data, and that this data is put into a format that is organized and easy to read. You will need to use these two keywords in order to determine what kind of data is going to show up.

The clause SELECT is going to introduce the different columns that you need to see with the search results, and then you need to work with the clause of FROM to find the exact points in the table that you need at this point.

FROM

We just mentioned the FROM clause a bit before, but it is important to spread it out into its own place. Remember from before that the SELECT and the FROM clause all need to work together to get the query done the way that you would like. The reason that both of these must show up together is that it takes the search from doing the whole database, down to just the actual things that you want to find in the database.

If you went through and did the query without the help of both of these clauses together, it is likely that you would have to search through all of the results that were in the database. If the business only had twenty items for sale altogether, then this may not be that big of a deal. But if they have a million items for sale, it is not likely that the customer, or even you, will want to sort through all of the results until you were able to find the one that you wanted.

When the SELECT and the FROM clause works together, you will find that this is no longer a problem. It will limit down the information that you need in the database, making it so that only the results that match up with the query are going to show up on the screen.

For this process to work, you need to have a minimum of one FROM clause. To help us learn a bit how this is going to work and how everything is going to come together with these two keywords, let's take a look at the syntax of an SQL code that will use both the FROM and SELECT keywords in the proper manner.

SELECT [*\ ALL| DISTINCT COLUMN1, COLUMN2]

FROM TABLE1 [, TABLE2]:

43

WHERE

The next keyword that we need to take a look at is the one WHERE. This is the one that you will need to use when you see more than one condition inside of the clause. A good example of this one is the element that shows up in the query that will display any of the data that is selective after the user has been able to put in any information they wish to find.

If you have decided to work with this kind of feature, there are going to be two other conditions that are proper to use here, and they include the OR and the AND operators. The best syntax to use to work with the WHERE command will include the following:

SELECT [\ALL\ DISTINCT COLUMN1, COLUMN2]*

FROM TABLE1 [, TABLE2]:

WHERE [CONDITION1 \ EXPRESSION 1]

[AND CONDITION2 \ EXPRESSION2]

ORDER BY

And the fourth clause that we are going to take a look at is the ORDER BY clause. You will be able to work this particular clause if it is time to arrange some of the output of the query that you did. The server is able to decide the format and the order of the information that the user will see when they are done with a basic query. If the user does not go through and determine the order type that they want, then the default for this will be to provide the output from A to Z.

This doesn't mean that you are stuck with this. You can go through and write out the information so that it shows up in any order that you would like, just make sure that it is done ahead of time if you want something other than the default. The syntax that you can use with this one will use the code that we wrote in the las last section, but then you need to add the line below to the end of it to make this work:

ORDER BY COLUMN1 | INTEGER [ASC/DESC]

All of these will need to be in place with your code if you would like to make sure that the command of SELECT is going to work in the proper manner and to ensure that it will be able to go through the database and pull out information that actually matches, or is similar, to the query you did about that database.

Working with the case sensitivity

The next topic that we need to take a look at is how case sensitivity is going to work with this language, and whether or not it is something that you need to worry about. The nice thing about working in the SQL language is that the case sensitivity is not going to matter as much, at least not as much as it does with some other coding languages that you can work with. You can choose to work with lower case and upper case letters, any of them that you would like because they will be viewed the same in any query that you do. You even get the choice of looking at the statements and the clauses and see the different ways that they will show up in the code.

Now, with this information said, there may be a few times in this language was the case sensitivity is going to be important. For example, you may have a time when you are in a situation where there are some data objects. You find that mostly, the data that you plan to use is all written out using upper case letters.

The reason that this happens is that it is done to let other users see something is consistent in the code, and they will know why. If you add in any other objects to that database, it is often best if you are able to list them out in upper case letters. Not because this is going to make that much of a difference, but it ensures that the information all look uniform and consistent.

Without this rule in place, may find that someone would get onto the database and use the term JOHN one time, but then another user would come on and use John, and then a third would go with john and so on. A beginner who is working on this language may run into trouble understanding whether these are the same thing or not, or if the users are talking about the same person here and this gets a bit confusing.

In the long run, it is better to have it all in uppercase letters in the code so that it matches, and it can make sure that everyone is always on the same page when it comes to using this kind of code. It also helps to prevent some potential issues that could come up otherwise.

The reason that those who developed SQL decided to work with the uppercase format, rather than something else, is because the uppercase letters are easier to read, and it is going to match up with what you may have done in some of the other databases that you may have done in the past. If you choose that the uppercase method is not really the best one for you, then at least make sure that your labeling and naming system is as consistent as possible to avoid some issues.

Another thing that we need to consider when we are working with some transactions in our database is that you will do a lot of queries and transactions with all of this as well. We talked about some of these before, but it is possible that the queries and the transactions are going to go together in some cases. These transactions are going to be important, although you may feel that this includes information that the user is not that interested in.

However, if you find that the case sensitivity is not used properly, or you don't take the time to check that the table is set up in the manner that you should have it, then you will end up with the results being wrong after the query. And this leads to unhappy customers who will not want to come back and check out your website ever again.

Any time that you decide to create a new database, and you want to work inside of it, you need to make sure that you have set up the query as well as possible ahead of time. This takes a few extra minutes when you are doing this, but it makes it so much easier for the user to find whatever they are looking for inside of your database. No one wants to come to your website and then find that it is too hard to get the information that they need. And working with the case sensitivity in the proper manner can sometimes be the reason that the code is not working the way that you would like.

Let's pretend that you are going to one of your favorite sights to look up some items that you would like to get. You have an idea of what you want, and you type it into the search query. How do you feel when you are able to find the right item that you want, with all of the right specifications, within the first few results that come up on the page? It is likely that you feel good and are appreciative that it doesn't take as much of your time to do this. You may even be more likely to come back to the website again and make another purchase.

On the other hand, how are you going to feel if you do the same thing, but the results come back nothing as you want? You try out four or five different keywords along the way, and nothing is matching up the way that you want. You look through pages of information, and it still doesn't give you the results that you want. When this happens, it is easy to get frustrated and mad, and you may get upset with the company and not want to work with them again.

This is the same idea when we are working with case sensitivity and getting this language to work with what you want. You are in business to make the customers happy, and if they are unhappy because your database is not working in the manner that you would like, then this is going to be a big problem that you need to fix.

This is why working with the queries that you need and making sure that they end up working in the proper manner and communicating with the database in the right manner is critical to ensuring the website works and that your customers are happy. Your ultimate goal here is that when the user visits your website and types in some kind of keyword for a search, that they are only getting items that closely match, and nothing else. This helps to make sure that the customer is going to be happy, and can help to build up your reputation as a business.

There are many people who will work with this kind of database to help them list out the products that they want customers to purchase. Even if this is the way that you plan on working on this database, there may still be some times when the search function could be useful, and you still want to make sure that it is functioning properly.

For example, if the user wants to come to your website, and they wish to look through the database and find specific information, such as their account information or the payment method that they like to use, or even the services you provide, it is still important that you have the query search set up in such a manner that this search is easy and that the user will find the information, even if they may not use the query as much as some other options.

As someone who is just getting started with the SQL language, it is important to realize how important some of these queries are and why you want to make sure that the SQL query is going to show up where it belongs, rather than giving a lot of information that the user does not need. No matter how you are using the database, these queries are going to be an integral part of the work that you are doing.

Chapter 6: Relational Database Concepts

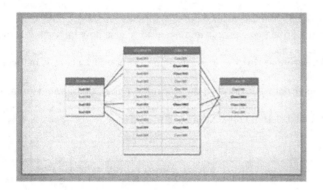

The next thing that we are going to explore when it comes to working with the SQL language is the idea of the relational database. The database engine that powers SQL is going to be strong, and it does have the ability to make decisions on its own, without the programmer there, thanks to the user-input instructions. The language of SQL, which is called Transact-SQL (also known as T-SQL) will contain some of the basic objects that are needed to define these data requests.

Literal values are going to be constant in your code, no matter what you are doing, and you may find that they will include numeric, hex, or alphanumeric values that will be turned into a string and enclosed into some single quotes. It is possible that you will need to work with double quotes here, but there are other uses for these quotes other than using this, and most coders are going to just stick with the single quotations to make things easier.

We also need to look at the delimited identifiers. These are there because inside of the code they will reserve specific keywords, while also enabling the objects of the database to contain names that include a space in them. The default that we see with these kinds of statements are going to use the double quotes that we talked about before. However, manipulation of this kind of setting can happen if you use the SET statement.

In some instances, there may be a statement that the engine of the database will not need to process at all, and it is important to look at these as well. Notating the lines that the code doesn't need to process will include having an asterisk and the forward-slash on both sides of the lines. So an example of this would be something like /* this is a quote */ will render the text between the notation as a comment.

There are a lot of codes out there that are going to use the idea of the comments to help get things done. These are basically like little notes that show up in your code, that let you and other coders know what is happening in the code, but will not affect the work that is taking place. If you want to name a particular part of the code, or you want to leave a note for another coder about the code, then you would use the comments that you would like without having to worry about it ruining the code or hurting any of the queries that are set with the program either.

In this language, the identifiers are going to be used to reference some of the diverse resources that are present including the database, the objects, and the tables, providing users with a new shorthand method that they can use in order to request the complex data that is found in the query. Of course, there are going to be a specific syntax that you need to implement and define them properly.

The nice thing about working with these identifiers is that they will be able to add in some complexity to any query string that you do, simply because they can introduce the variable syntax rules. Identifiers can start with pretty much any kind of character that you would like. But once you have been able to set these, you need to make sure that the names are chosen carefully so that they won't be called out on accident. And like many of the other languages that are out there, there will be some reserved keywords, which have reserved meanings and can only be used to call up commands and actions inside of the language.

Creating data that you are able to reference back is going to mean that we need to adhere to certain processes and that some level of consistency needs to be present the whole time. This can happen when you limit the data that is inside of a column to just one type of data, and no more. Of course, there can always be exceptions to this based on the kind of program that you are trying to create, but for the most part, each column in the database or in a table needs to just have one single data type in it.

Numeric data is just fine in the database. Sometimes this is used to represent various forms of counted data including decimal, integer, real, and money depending on the program you are working with. All of these are numerical data and basically means that you will fill in that particular column of the database with some kind of number in the process.

You can then go with some character data containers. These are going to be available in both a variable and a fixed-length strip. If you want just to let the person put in the abbreviation for the state, then you would limit these containers to two parts. If you want to let them pick out a unique password, or you want them to write out their whole name without any restrictions, then you would use the variable character.

Then there are some of the Unicode store containers. These are going to take the character strings that have a byte that is bigger than one. Data related to time is going to be called temporal data, and it is important because it is able to concern date and time information that is stored in different sizes and with different specifics attached to each one. You will find that most of the data types that are temporal are not going to understand things like time zones or daylight savings time, but the DATETIMEOFFSET is able to define a type of data that is able to accommodate the time zones if it is needed to manipulate the data at hand.

You may find that this language will allow you to also work with different types of data that may not fit into the three categories that we were talking about at all. But they do still need to fit into some of the other parameters, including things like SQL-variant, large objects, and binary data to name a few.

Another thing that we need to take a look at here is how the SQL language is going to enlist two kinds of functions, which are known as the scalar and the aggregate. First, we will take a look at the aggregate function. As we can guess by the name, this data is going to be contained within one single column, and because of this, it is going to return just one value for the query. It is possible to work with several types of these functions, including user-defined, analytical, statistical, and convenient.

An example of working with the aggregate function is going to be when we use the SUM function. This SUM function is going to calculate out the total value of all the entries that you are able to find in a single column. This function, in particular, is going to be known as a convenient function, and the complexity of what you are able to do with this is going to be staggering when you form queries that can apply some of the other functions, especially when we take a look at what this is able to do with some of the user-defined aggregate functions.

Then we need to take a look at the scalar functions. These are going to be divided up into five categories, and they will operate on a single row or a singular value as opposed to an aggregate function which will run on many rows inside just one column. There are actually hundreds of these functions that can come into use when we talk

51

about data manipulation, but to keep it simple we will break them down into metadata, system, string, date, and numeric functions.

Functions are going to manipulate the data, and then the numeric functions are able to transform the data using some of the instructions that are mathematical. The date functions are able to perform some calculations on the date and the time of your formulated data. And then we have the string function which is going to include things like shaping character string data.

We can then take a look at the system functions that are a bit more varied than what we find with other options, and these are going to provide us with some information about the objects that are found in the database. These functions are not going to be able to take the data and transform it as much as some of the other options, but they are important because they will give us the information that we need to figure out the state of our database and how this database is doing.

And finally, we need to take a look at the metadata functions. This is also going to follow this form while providing us information regarding the state of our database. These functions are going to help us by retrieving all of the names and the IDs of objects in the database. You will see that things like data types, tables, views, schemas, databases, and database files are going to be the primary concern when it comes to the metadata functions. In some cases, you are able to use this kind of function to allow for the retrieval of values for a given property without the objects of the database, within the database itself, or even in the instance of the server.

Operators that are inside this language are going to be scalar, and they will be able to apply to the mathematical and the Boolean operations, including the concatenation. Concatenation is going to be a database context that is meant to refer back to the joining together of many tables, fields, or objects. Operator types that fall into this can include binary and unary arithmetic, bitwise, set operators, logic operators, compound, comparison, and more.

Of course, we need to have a look at some of the operators that are used here to make sure that we can manipulate the data as we want. Some of the symbols that help us to do this manipulation will include OR, NOT, and AND. These can work on any function across all of the types of data that you want to work with.

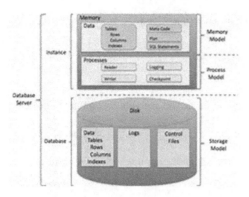

We are not going to be able to list out all of the operators that are available with this because there are too many to include without getting too technical with this work and most of the models and their usage are going to be beyond the scope of what we are trying to do with this book. The most important thing to note with this is that there are a lot of possibilities that you can consider and as familiarity with this language increases, encountering some of the operators that are seen as the most common will happen all of the time.

If you need to learn a bit more about how these operators work and how you can make sure that you get the most out of it, you will find that both ORACLE and Microsoft are going to present us with some free education about these operators and how to use them the way that you need.

The next things that we need to take a look at are the NULL values and the global variables. These are going to require some inclusion into some of the more essential components of SQL. First, we will look at the global variables. These are going to be used in place of the constants in the code, and you will need to proceed them by @@ to show that a global variable is inserted there.

NULL values are also going to be a significant feature of working in SQL. Even though relational meddles are going to require that all data is referenceable in the real world practice, there are times when some unknown data is going to show up, and the NULL value allows you to create a table still, and manipulate it the way that you would like, without all of the information in the table is present each time.

Understanding the basics of this languages data type functions and the objects will provide a base of knowledge that will expand into the progressively more specific areas of database creation and manipulation.

Going through this chapter and looking through what each of these parts is in this chapter to help you get the results that you want with this coding.

Chapter 7: How to Define Data in SQL

The next thing that we need to focus on when it comes to SQL is how to define some of the data that we are using in SQL. Defining the databases means that we need to be able to use the right statements in this language that relates back to the data definition language. Operations that are related to deletion, modification, and creation are the three segments of this kind of language that we need to look through.

To start, the organization of our database is going to comprise of many different types of objects. You can have either logical or physical objects based on the data that you are working with and the device that the user is working with as well. And even though it can seem a bit redundant, the database is going to be part of the organization of the database. What this means is that the database itself is one of the objects that we can work with, and when the right statement is used, you will be able to manipulate this object as well.

Of course, it is impossible to go through and work with a database if you don't first have a database object in place first. And the two main methods that you can use to make this happen include CREATE DATABASE, or you can even work with the SQL management studio if you are working with this language on a Microsoft product. The Oracle version is going to function in a slightly different manner, but it is still pretty straightforward to work with as well.

As you are creating a new database, remember that you need to name the database. This is going to make sure that the engine is going to be able to use this identifier to call up the database any time there is a query going on for that information. The name needs to follow the same kinds of restrictions that all of the other identifiers are going to share as we talked about before.

As you create a database, you will find that it will define the creator as the owner of the database, and then it goes through and also makes a log file that is able to track each change that is made to the database, from the moment it is created onward. Even if logging is not correctly defined yet, the system is able to generate a log file to help maintain the changes that you end up doing, mainly for the benefit of the engine of the database's logic.

Earlier in this guidebook, we talked about the data independence specified that the functionality of a database is not dependent on the logical or the physical structure. This is why it is so important to impart that the function is not going to be affected by how data is stored and accessed on the physical disk. Physical data organization does end up affecting the performance in some situations, such as when the database is really extensive.

When the database is extensive, the established methodologies are going to exist in order to create some filegroups of related databases for distribution among various physical disks to enhance how well it is able to perform.

The creation of a new database is going to allow for a template called a model. The usage of models is going to occur when a specific element or object in the database has to be present in all of the databases that you create. This is going to be set by the administrator and isn't always a necessity. The SQL database is also going to allow for a snapshot view of the database at a given interval in time if this is needed. The reason that some companies like to work with snapshots is that it is really useful to help you protect your database against any of the errors that your users may have, as well as to help you understand some of the evolution that happens in the code.

Any of the elements that are considered primary elements will be found inside the tables of the database. Your tables are going to require that you use consistent integrity in the data to make sure that it stays stable. The administrators are going to be the part of the database that comes in and maintain the consistency, but you will find that the engine for the database will provide the administrator with some tools to create any limitations to prevent some of the inconsistent entries users may do.

This is why you need to work with the database engine in a consistent manner. This feature is vital because even the administrators are going to be susceptible to some human error, but the database engine is going to be immune to some of the limitations of human error. It is possible to turn on some of these restrictions and then turn it over to the management system, either on a table wide or a per column basis based on what seems to work the best for the database you are creating.

Examples of table or column restrictions could include requiring unique clauses to identify candidate keys, and one of those potential columns is eligible to become the primary key. The primary key is going to be a column where each row of the column will contain a different value from the others. This is going to be considered the most important column in the whole table, and this will need to be set up as the basis of querying specific information based on the unique identifiers for a given database.

Foreign keys can show up as well, and these are going to be the matching identifier to a primary key, but it is going to be in a related, but a separate database. These two fields must maintain data consistency in order also to maintain their integrity. The check clause is going to help the data entry users to retain reference agreement by enforcing requirements upon insertion of new data.

The transact language in SQL is going to support you modify the structure of database objects, and some of the ones that you can modify will include the database, the table, the procedure, view, trigger, and schema. Adding or removing any of the logs in the filegroups or the files of the database is something that you will do the most option, but there are other things that you are able to do with this. SQL is going to store each of the databases on a single disk file, and the filegroup is just going to be a larger collection of these files.

Modifying the database using this method is helpful in some cases because it is going to enhance how well it performs, and can even change up some of the physical storage structure that comes with the data, without having to change up the execution of the queries. You can also choose to edit a database with the code ALTER DATABASE clause, and this statement is also responsible for setting the database options or changing the properties of the filegroup.

The database options available are going to be varied, and they will include things like a change of the state of the database including who can access it, the people who can read or write on the database, the status of access such as whether you can get it offline or only online and more. The SQL language is going to allow you to have a moving database with the help of the command for attaching and detach, but while you are able to do this, there are a lot of issues that can come up with the process.

The good news is that while that process can run you into some issues if you are not careful, Microsoft has come up with a contained database to help deal with the loss of metadata that sometimes happens with detachment. Detaching the database is going to help retain the information that you need, but then the security and the properties of the database are going to be considered separate from the data. What this resulted in was that in the past, when you moved a database, it would require a tedious amount of rebuilding the security and some of the metadata that went missing.

Thanks to the contained database that is available with Microsoft now, you are able to move the database and all of the attributes that come with it, quickly and effectively. The SQL Server 2012 is only going to support a partially contained database, but the newer versions from 2014 and on are able to have the contained database, and this is going to be a process that is similar to creating the objects of your objects.

The neat thing that comes up here is that the commands are going to be simple. All of the commands that you used for the CREATE statement will exist in duplicate when you decide to use the DROP statement in the code. But one critical aspect of dropping the objects of the database to remember is that it includes losing the data, the triggers, and the indices that are related to any of the discarded data.

Retention of the views of that database will remain dependent on the presence of the data. The "View" will then be incomplete at this point because the reference data no longer needs to exist, but you will find that the "View" is still selectable in this situation.

From here, we need to take a look at a few of the data definition statements, and in particular we need to look at the ones like ALLOW, DROP, and CREATE and how these are going to be responsible for the creation of new procedures, indices, triggers schema, views, tables, and even with new databases.

First, we have the ALTER statement for objects. This one is going to be robust when we take a look at all that it is able to accomplish, and it is going to be helpful when you would like to define the functionality of a database. There are a lot of different things that you are able to do with this statement that we won't have time for in this guidebook, but it is still important to know that the ALTER statement is going to be a good one for you to learn how to use when it comes to the functionality of the tables you are working on.

Chapter 8: Working with Indexing, Views, and Queries

Now that we have had a chance to take a look at some of the different things that you are able to work on in the SQL language, and some of the background noise that helps to make sure the database is able to work, it is time for us to explore a bit more about some of the actual actions that you are able to work with when you want to make this coding language work for you.

It is all well and good to create some of the databases and put in the information that you need along the way. You won't be able to do anything with the database if there is not a strong table and good information put into it as well. But you may find that this process is not going to do all of the things that you want until you learn how to work with a few other actions.

In this guidebook, we are going to take a look at doing queries, views, and indexing with the codes that you want to write in SQL. These are all going to be a bit different from each other, but it is something that you and the user will need to use on a regular basis to actually use and access the database that has been created. So, let's get started.

The first option that we need to take a look at queries here. These queries are simple to work with because they will work with one single statement in order to get the retrieval of the data that is needed, and that statement is SELECT. This statement is one that we have talked about a bit before in this guidebook, but it is a good idea to have some review of how it works and why it is such an important part of any code that you decide to write.

Remember that the select statement includes a few different parts of the code that you need including operators, functions, and clauses.

Now, there are a lot of options when it comes to expanding out one of the queries that you are writing, and in some queries, this can make the search a bit more complex. What we mean by complex queries here is that they are going to have a lot of different parts to them. Instead of working with just "girl's dresses" for your query, for example, you may decide to add in the color, the length, how long it takes to ship, and the size and turn it into a more complex query.

SELECT statements are going to request for information from one or more table that is inside the database, or that are inside more than one database at the time. The results of a query return in a table format, which makes sure that you or the user will receive a new database table called the result set. Some of the clauses that you will be able to use when you decide to do a query will include ORDER BY, HAVING, GROUP BY, WHERE, FROM, and INTO.

We will start by looking at the WHERE clause. This one is important because it is going to define any of the conditions that will limit the rows of data that you can select. It operates more as a Boolean function where the resultant set is returned based on whether the statement is true or false, and will check the rows that you specified to find it in the first place. This clause uses Boolean results because this is going to allow for a bit more complexity by being able to add in another operator to the mix, including AND, NOT, and OR following some of the standard logic that is Boolean.

The operators also have some weights that are prioritized in the order of NOT, AND, then OR, and this is going to be important when you want to apply some logic to one of the queries that you are working on. We can then move on to some operators that are not considered Boolean, and these are going to be BETWEEN and IN, can work in conjunction with the Boolean operators to help you to delineate some of the requests that you have for the data.

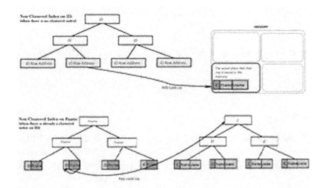

When you are doing some of the work to design these queries, it is useful to help you write the query in plain language as much as possible, and then you can translate that everyday speech into logic. Another of the non-Boolean operators that you may work with, LIKE, is going to be able to tell the engine of the database to seek patterns within a column and return results based on some of the other operators that work in conjunction with it.

Then there is the clause of GROUP BY which allows for some column data to be grouped in a manner so that the query can return similar rows of data where the grouped columns end up holding onto the same type of data. Then the HAVING clause is going to be applied when groups of rows require a condition to recover data within the syntax of a query to help you out. This is often either going to be an aggregate function or a constant value, such as the sum of the columns altogether. All of the clauses of this are going to be built upon one another to increase the complexity. The logic of the HAVING clause here is going to be that it specifies a value in order to delineate information by when the GROUP BY clause returns a larger resultant set than desired.

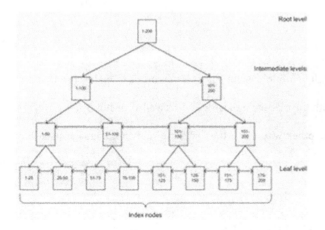

The HAVING clause is going to limit the specific data that is going to come up when you use GROUP BY into a particular limit on that data or for that comparison of data.

We can then move over to the ORDER BY clause which is going to specify the way that the data needs to be returned when the query is done and allows for the information to show up for the user in a manner that makes the most sense. It could do something like the lowest price to highest, or even from ascending or descending order based on what you would like. It is possible for you to go through and modify the priority of the columns that are displayed, which would then allow you to change the order from the SELECT statement, or even sort the data by multiple columns at the same time.

While it may seem like these statements are confusing and that they will be too confusing when you try to work on them at the same time. But some examples that we will look at in a bit will help to clarify the situation and will make sure that we can fully use them all in the proper manner and still get the most that we can from them.

These queries are going to be important to work with because they are important for sorting through a lot of tables and databases, while getting through a ton of data that is found in them, in a quick and efficient manner. How fast they are able to do this will depend on the size and the arrangement of the database of course. If you have millions of results, it could take a bit longer for the program to actually go through the database and find the information that you want. Of course, you do have some methods available to make sure that the time it takes the system to respond is kept to a minimum. The best way to do this is to index the data so that it can be accessed faster.

The database engine is going to try to work with an optimizer for the query in order to make sure that any results it is providing are achieved more quickly with the existing indices in use, as well as deciding if some of the indexed data has been moved or modified in any other way since the last time that the language used any statements to drop, alter, or create the indexes.

If this process is done and a table is not attached, then the system is going to go through each part of the database, line for line and column for the column, in order to find the results that go with the query. As you can imagine, this is not going to really help you much because the process is tedious and can take too long. But while it is not efficient, the data is going to be processed quickly so that when the database is relatively small, the slowdown is something that you can manage.

Basically, you want to find the best way to index your database to ensure that when a query is done, it is going to be done in a manner that makes sense for the user, and the slowdown speed of that method is not really going to be that noticeable to move people.

Rows that are indexed within the index page are going to contain what is known as a pointer and an index key that will allow the database engine to scan the page more quickly, rather than trying to scan the whole table and determine the kind of data that is the most relevant. This can make it more efficient and works the best when you have large pieces of data that you need to sort through. The data structure that is found within one of these indexes is going to follow the B-tree organization.

What is a B-tree? These are going to be a self-balancing data structure that is able to sort through the data and allows for queries, insertions, deletions, and insertions of information in the form of keys, along with some other parent and child leaves as needed. The indices will take two different forms when you are working with them in SQL, and the two forms are going to include non-clustered and clustered.

First, we need to take a look at the clustered indexes. These are the ones that are going to determine the physical order of the data that is found in the table. Only one of these types can exist per table because it is physically impossible to order data in more than one way.

From there, the leaf nodes are going to contain the data pages, while the rest of the tree that you are able to find will comprise of the index pages pointing to where the relevant data locations are within the nested structure. Now, there are also indexes that are known as non-clustered, and these come in pretty much the same kind of structure that we talked about before, but there are two main differences that we have to know that sets these apart.

First, when you are working with a non-clustered index, you will notice that it is not going to be able to actually change the physical location where you find data in the table, and then the leaf page that comes with this is not going to contain any of the actual data that you are going to use. Instead of all this, the leaves are basically like bookmarks in the code and the index keys. These bookmarks are important to the code because they will make the database more efficient and will provide a direct shortcut to your queried data.

It is possible to have some of these non-clustered parts work at the same time as the clustered indexes, but it is also possible that they may work on their own when you bring them into a database. It all depends on the kind of program that you are trying to create for your needs.

At times, you will find that these indexes are going to become more fragmented with use from you. The more times that the data is retrieved and then stored again, it is possible that this is done in a manner that is not that efficient, and things start to break up and become fragmented. Taking some time on occasion to reorganize the information is a good option any time that you fear the fragmentation of the data is more severe. Indexing is a vital part of your database and can make sure that the code is going to work the way that you would like to see it work.

Another core competency that we need to take a moment to study here is all about creating and then leveraging the views that you have. To keep this as simple as possible, the view is going to be another name that we are going to give for a virtual table. A base table is always going to exist inside of your physical store, but then you can also have a virtual table, as long as you make sure that you do not index it and you make sure that it doesn't take up any storage in your data.

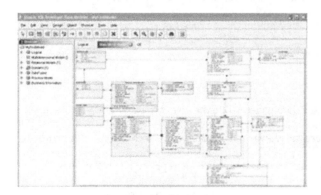

Views are going to be a kind of object that is found in the database, and you will see that it is derived from some of the base tables thanks to the help of the metadata that we talked about before. The creation of a new view can source from a separate virtual table, but there are a few reasons that make it beneficial to create one of your one.

You will find that sometimes, a query is going to be a bit more complicated, and you can simplify these with the help of a virtual table that is able to correspond back to the query for the database, the one that you or another user typed in, to begin with. The relationship that is going to show up here can reveal an important fact that we need to look at with views and this is that the views are going to come from a resultant set of data that is then returned by the query that was used.

A good way to help with this issue is to try and limit the scope of the values that your users are able to modify and update can be another reason here. If you make it so that each user is only able to create or change certain parts of the database, rather than the whole thing, you prevent someone from just coming in and messing up the database, and you also make sure that human error when it comes to importing data into your database, will be kept away, or at least down to a minimum.

Queries are going to be an important part of any coding that you do in the SQL database. You will find that a lot of people are going to want to master this skill because it allows them to make sure that everything comes up in the right manner. There is no way that you or one of your users will want to actually go through and manually read through all of the results that come with your database, but when the query is set up the right way, then this ensures that the right results come up each time.

With this in mind, we talk about indexes. These are basically going to help leave a little bookmark behind so that the query is able to find the information that it needs as well. They may not be necessary, but when you are working with an SQL database that is relatively big in size, it can make the search more efficient and more accurate overall, so it is definitely worth your time to learn how to use these as well.

This chapter has contained a lot of the information that we need to know in order to create some of the best codes for our needs. But there is definitely a lot of new information to go through and taking the time to check out all of the things that you are able to do with the SQL language, and how you can work with some of the databases that are found with this one can make a world of difference as well.

As we talked about in this guidebook a little bit, creating queries, leveraging, indexing, and establishing some pertinent views that make sense from a business intelligence perspective are really a big core component that comes with those who want to work with SQL. There is so much that you are able to do with the help of this kind of database, and it helps to keep all of your information so organized, that it makes sense to have it as part of your own business organization as well.

Of course, since we have gone through a lot of different topics during this chapter, it is also natural to feel a bit overwhelmed and like this is a lot of information to take in! The best way to master these skills is to work on them a bit and practice. SQLite is an application that you are able to get for free that will make sure that a new user to SQL is able to get started easily and gain some of the experience that you need to really see what the database is able to do on its own.

Chapter 9: Database Security

As you work with some of the databases that your business needs, you will find that the topic of security is going to come up. You have to make sure that you are able to give your customers the security that they need. They are not going to be all that happy if you decide to work on their information and you ask them to store it with you, but then you are not able to keep the information that they provide to you safely.

Think about all of the personal information that a business could hold onto for their customers. If you have a customer who makes a purchase with you and saves their information into an account, it is likely that you have some information including their name, address, phone number, and credit card number to name a few. This may not seem like that big of a deal because this is the information that the customer had to provide to you to complete the purchase. But if this information gets into the wrong hands, it could be a big headache for the customer, and the end of your business for you.

It is your job to make sure that any time you have a database that stores your customers' information for them that you are doing whatever you can to keep the information private and secure. But how are you supposed to use SQL to make sure that this security is in place over the database?

Databases are going to be containers that are able to maintain all kinds of data, corporate secrets, employee data that is sensitive, list of employees that are scheduled out for separation, customer payment information, and other types of information that no one outside of the company should really have access too. It is common for many companies to use Microsoft's active directory to help them manage users and to sort them into access profiles using a group them into a group policy process.

The way that this works in practice, and when it is used properly, is that the employees of a company are going to be given an assigned group permission based on the job title that they have, and within those permissions, there is also the possibility for more individualized permissions depending on the rank that the employee has in the group. This ensures that the company is able to control who gets to do what based on their position and ranking within the company.

You will see that the SQL is going to interact back with the Active Directory for some of the access control, but it is not going to be able to provide any internal security when it comes to the authorization. The application that comes with SQL is going to provide these services for you. As we go through this, you will notice that with the SQL database, there are going to be four main components that come into play with database security. And these are going to include authentication, authorization, encryption, and access control. Let's take a look at each of these to see how they are able to help us out when it comes to the security of our database.

First on the list is the authentication. This is going to pertain to validating whether or not a user has the right permissions to access any of the resources that are on the system in the first place. One of the most common methods that you may see when it comes to authentication is going to be the idea of the username and password.

You will then be able to verify the credentials by the username and the password to determine if the user is supposed to be on the system or not.

There is a lot of potentials that can come with this method. The company gets some freedom on the rules for the username and passwords to add in a new layer of security as well. You can also choose to go with a single sign-on system if you would like. These systems are going to use the idea of certificate authentication that the user is not actually going to interact within a direct manner. The end-user will find that their system is prepared to deal with the information that provides authentication automatically, without needing to have a prompt come up or the user to do anything.

As you can imagine, many companies are going to take great steps to make sure that their system and who is able to access it, is going to be authenticated and appropriately authorized all of the time. Then the encryption is going to help make sure that this access control is strengthened a bit more because it scrambles the data into indecipherable gibberish to any potential interceptors as the data is moved between the company and the user.

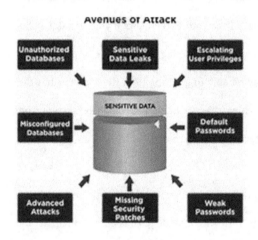

There are different types of encryption that can be used on the program, but for Microsoft, you will find that the RSA encryption type is going to be used in order to protect the data. This RSA is going to be an encryption algorithm that is going to use a layered hierarchical structure along with key management in order to secure data as needed.

It is important to have both of these parts present in the authentication process. The first one will ensure that any user who is trying to get onto the database is supposed to do so. The second one makes sure that the information that is sent over to the user is going just to reach them, and won't get intercepted along the way. This is the best way to make sure that the data stays between the company and the user who requested it.

The second part of database security that we need to take a look at includes the authorization. This is going to be a process that is used in order to determine which resources that are in the system are accessible by the user. Once the client has been able to provide the right credentials, the next step is to decide which entities the subject has permission to modify or access.

Just because a user has a password and username doesn't mean that they can access every part of the system. Usually, they are going to be restricted to the information that directly pertains back to them, but they wouldn't be allowed to access the information of someone else's account unless they were the administrator. This helps to make sure that users are only able to see the information that pertains to them, and to no one else, and can keep the information as secure as possible.

In addition, SQL is going to use change tracking to maintain a good log of all the actions that could potentially come from unauthorized users. It is possible to track the activities of the authorized users if you would like, but this isn't really a part of the security functionality that comes with change tracking. Super-users or power-users that have elevated permissions could have more access and may be able to get into all of the systems, but this doesn't necessarily authorize them as users of the database. Tracking changes helps to protect the system from any operations that may be done by users who have more elevated credentials than other users.

SQL is going to rely on a security model that is comprised of three models, and all three of these models are able to interplay with one another. The three models that you can work with include permissions, principals, and securable the first one that we need to focus on here is going to be the principals. These users are going to have permission in order to access some specific objects in the system. Then the securable will refer to any of the resources that are within the database that the system is going to regulate the access of and only certain users are able to get to it. And then there is the idea of permission that is the right of a user to delete, edit, or view some of the other parts. The permission is usually either limited, yes, or no.

This is a security model that belongs to the Microsoft SQL Server, but there are going to be similar equivalents that are found on other versions of SQL management products. The theories behind modeling access control are going to be widespread through the IT industry, and they have been designed in a way that will cover much more than just the security of the database. These are some of the same principles that you are able to find behind nearly all of the enterprise applications that are going to house some sensitive data.

The security that comes with the database you use is so important. It doesn't really matter the version of SQL that you choose to work with. They all require that you have some form of security that comes with them, and this will ensure that you get the results that you want because companies want to make sure that their information is safe and that no one who doesn't have access to the account is able to get ahold of it.

Security is an important subject when it comes to the SQL database, and many companies are trying to find new ways that they are able to maintain this kind of security when they work on the database. There are a lot of books out there to talk about how to make this security even stronger, but the goal of this chapter is to do some of the most relevant topics to help you learn why the security is so important, and how you can make sure that the security is as strong as possible.

To start here, we talked about the schema a bit in some of the previous chapters, but this is also going to be something that is important for helping to define the ownership of the resources, and it can identify the principals by deciding how the user is related back to the owner. To keep this easy, the way that Microsoft defines the schema is going to be "a collection of database objects that are owned by a single person and form a single namespace."

It is important to know about the namespace because it is going to refer to the limitation that doesn't allow two tables in the same schema to go in with the same name. Data consistency and the referential ease are going to be some of the guiding ideas that come in with the design of SQL, and this is why we need to have some of the limitations in place.

It is possible to have a principal that is a single user or a single login, but it is also possible to have them be designed as a group principle. Multiple users who are sharing one role are going to be grouped together using group policy, and all can cooperatively own a schema, or they could each of their own and add all of these schemas to the same account.

It is also possible for you to take a schema and transfer it from one principle to another. When you decide to do this, it is not going to require you to rename unless the new owners maintain a schema that would end up with a duplication in the name. There are statements in this language that are meant to manage the schema, but a majority of this is going to belong back to the database administrators, rather than the principles on that system.

Another layer of security that you are able to work with will be the roles. These are used in order to identify access dependent on the title of the user and their responsibilities. There are going to be a lot of choices when it comes to the roles that are available. SQL comes with fixed server roles and a fixed role in the database, which will provide you with some implicit permissions that you do not even need to set because they will do the work for you.

Another thing that you can do here is to go through and create some of the customized application roles that you want, user-defined server roles, and even user-defined database roles. It all depends on what kind of roles you would like to see inside of your system, and what makes the most sense for your business.

These roles are going to make sure that the right users are doing the tasks that they need to within the program. If someone has a lower role in the company, for example, some of their access to the system is going to be more restricted. They may be able to view the system, but wouldn't be able to make changes to the system, or they will only be allowed in certain parts of the system. It all depends on how you set up the roles in your database.

As you can see with this one is that the roles are going to be an important part of the security that comes with your database. All of the other functions of security that you are going to try and work with will be built upon

73

these roles. Authentication is going to help us determine who is able to access the database. The authorization is going to determine which principles have access to each schema. Then we have the encryption which will ensure that data sent between the user and the system is not intercepted from those who are outside of the company. This can also help to make sure that no potential hazards happen internally in the system either.

Sensitive data that leaks internally or that is intercepted unintentionally is going to be more dangerous than some of the external threats that are out there. This is why the roles are so important because they will maintain the information about which users are allowed to perform any given operation within a particular database.

If you are using the version of SQL that comes with Microsoft, you will find that this version is going to teach some of the security principals that are going to provide the user with the least amount of access that is possible while still letting them do their duties. This means that you will not give the user any more access to the system than they need because this ensures that no one is gaining more access than they need and prevents some security issues. If the person doesn't need access to something to do their job, then there is no reason for them to have access to it and this teaching will say that you restrict that to keep the system as safe as possible.

This kind of theory is going to prevent users from having any access to resources that they don't need to use and that they are not really trained to use. The same guiding ideas are going to be used when you work with all of the other versions of SQL as well. The purpose of the roles as we have discussed in this chapter is to limit the amount of access an employee has to the database that does not actually pertain to the work or responsibilities that they have inside of that schema.

In this system, the owners are going to be seen as "sysadmins," but all of the users of the database are going to end up with some specialized functions based on their training and some of the experience that they have.

To make sure that the security is properly in place inside of the system, the database administrators are often going to be a part of the IT department. This allows them to routinely check on the database and make sure that everything is working the way that it should and that nothing strange is going on, every employee or user is on the system in the right manner, and that no threats are present in the system.

While the database administrators are going to be part of the company's IT department, the owners of the database are not usually found in this department. This allows for a level of autonomy, which is actually necessary because administrators are going to be responsible for maintaining the structure and the consistency of many different databases, the number of which depends on the size of the company and what they are trying to do. These roles and these rules are all there for the end goal of making sure that the database is as secure and consistent as possible.

Security is going to be so important when you are working with one of your own databases in your company. You want to make sure that only the right people are able to get the information that they need, and that no one is stealing the information or gaining access to information and to the system when they have to no reason to be there at all.

The way that you do the security is going to depend on the type of system and database that you are using, and who you would like to have on the system doing each task. The best theory to go with to ensure that only the right people are going to gain access to the different parts of the database is to make sure that they only access the amount of the system that they need in order to get their job done, and nothing more.

This can make it seem harsh, and sometimes it may be a pain always to have to change up the roles and the authorization that you will allow the employee to have when they are on the system, but it is going to make a big difference in the security that is present. You will be able to change things up as you want if roles and responsibilities end up changing, but limiting some of this is going to be the safest and most secure bet.

In addition, when you create a new database for your business, it is always a good idea to set up a username and password protocol that your employees are able to pick. Make sure though that there are some rules to add to the security. You don't want someone in the company to pick out a password that is easy to guess and can compromise the whole system. Having them stick with a minimum number of characters, asking them to have a mixture of symbols, numbers, and letters can help, and even requiring a password change a few times a year can help to keep the information as safe as possible.

While talking about the database security with your IT department, make sure that you discuss the idea of encryption with them. You do not want the information to end up going over to an authorized user, to find out that someone outside of the system was able to read all of that confidential information. The right encryption is going to ensure that the information gets jumbled up and impossible to read so that only the user who is supposed to have that information will be the one who is able to read that information.

As you can see, there are a number of different methods that you are able to use when it comes to making sure that your database is as safe and secure as possible with the SQL coding language. Doing this and getting everything organized, ensuring the right authorizations are in place, and limiting how much information an individual user is able to see will ensure that your database is going to stay as safe and secure as possible.

Chapter 10: How to Use This in Real-World Situations

Now that we have taken some time to look at the SQL database, and some of the different codes and more that you are able to do with this system, it is time to take a more practical approach to this. It is time to take a look at some of the ways that you are able to use SQL in the real world, and how this can benefit your business and more.

When we look at some of the practical situations, it is common to set that databases are going to be used by more than one user, and this is often at the same time. A database that is able to support many users at once has a high level of concurrency within it. This concurrency, in some cases, will be able to lead to a loss of data or the reading of data that is not really present.

Database Architecture

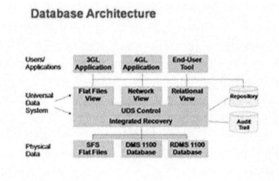

This can be a big issue to deal with depending on the kind of database that you are using. SQL is great because it is going to manage these kinds of situations with the help of transactions to control things like the durability, isolation, consistency, and atomicity that comes in some databases over time. These elements are going to comprise all of the properties that you need to look at during the transaction.

This brings up the question of what the transaction is going to be. This transaction is going to basically be a sequence of T-SQL statements that are going to combine logically and then are able to complete an operation that, in other situations, would introduce inconsistency to the database. Atomicity is a property that acts as a container for these transaction statements as you work on this. If the statement is able to successfully complete their work, then the total transaction is going to be completed.

For the most part, SQL is successful with the work that they are going to do, but if there is some part of the transaction that, for one reason or another, is not able to process fully, then the whole of the operation is going to fail, and all of the partial changes that showed up are going to head back to their previous state so you don't end up with issues or mistakes that happen.

Transactions are going to take place once a row, or they can be in a page-wide lock is in place. Locking is important because it is going to make sure that other users are not able to come into the database and make modifications to that particular part of the database. It is basically the same as reserving some spots inside of your database to make changes.

If you have locked that part of the database and the user then goes through and tries to change the data that is under the lock, the process is going to end up ailing, and then they will see a communication come up that the object in question is not available for them to modify at this time. This helps you to make some of the changes in the system more permanent so as to avoid overwriting and other issues along the way.

Transforming the data using transactions is important because it allows the database to move from one state that was consistent with a new state that is consistent. There are times when you would want to do this, but it is critical to understand that the transactions can modify more than one kind of database at a time.

If you do end up going through and changing some of the data in the database that is a foreign key or a primary key without also updating this information in the other locations, this is going to create data that is seen as inconsistent, and then the SQL system is not going to accept what you are trying to do here.

Transactions are going to be a really big part of changing related data from multiple-table sources all at the same time. The transactional transformation is going to help keep the isolation in place, a property that prevents concurrent transactions from interfering with one another. If you are looking at the database, and you see that two transactions are happening at the same time, you will see that only one of these transactions is going to be successful.

The transactions that are happening are going to remain invisible and will remain that way until you are able to get them to complete fully. Whichever of the transactions is able to get done first, that will be the one that the system accepts. The new information displays when it is completed, and when the failed transactions are done in that way. When it gets to this point, the user is going to need to decide if the updated information is going to require the modifications or not.

If a power outage were to occur, and you find that the system stability is going to fail, then the data durability is going to step up and will make sure that the effects of an incomplete transaction are able to roll back to their original state. This may not end up exactly where you want it at the end of things, but at least you don't lose all of the work that you have done in this.

When you get to a point where one of the transactions is able to complete, but then another of the transactions doesn't end up finishing, then it is going to retain the completed transaction. Rollbacks are something that can be accomplished by a database engine using the log of transactions to identify the previous state of the data and then move the transactions back to this, ensuring that you don't lose out on all of the work that you have been doing.

Now, it is important to realize that there are going to be a few different variations of the database lock, and even various properties of locks at the same time. To start with are the lock properties, and these are going to include properties that include duration, granularity, and mode.

We will take a look at the duration, and the easiest way that we are able to define this term is that it is the way that specifies a time interval where the lock has been applied. The lock mode will define different types of locking, and these modes can be determined based on the type of resource being locked.

A shared lock can come into play with this as well, and this will allow the data reads while the row or page lock is in effect. Then there are exclusive locks that are going to be useful when you want to work with DML or data manipulation, and these locks are going to provide you with exclusive use of a page or a row for the execution of any modification that you would like to do. Exclusive locks are not going to take place in a concurrent manner, as data is going to be modified in an active manner; the page is then going to be inaccessible to all of the other users of the system, no matter their responsibilities or roles.

Then we can move to the update locks. These kinds of locks are going to be placed onto just one object, and this allows for the reading of the data while the lock is in place. It is also helpful because it will let the database determine whether or not an exclusive lock is necessary once you modify the transaction. The update lock is pretty much the best of both worlds, allowing the reading of data and DML transactions to happen at the same time at least until you are committing the actual update in the table or in the row.

This update lock is going to allow you to work on just the one option that you want, or the one part of the database, without affecting the use of all the others. Someone is not going to really be able to do much with that object, but they can still view it and see what is going on with it. Then, when it is all organized, and you are ready to work with the modification, the exclusive lock will be in place, just for as long as that modification took.

These types of locks are going to be known as page-level locking, but there are other options that you can use. We are just going to spend time on these ones because they are the ones that you are most likely to work with when you set up an SQL database.

The final property of a lock that we need to take a look at is the granularity which is going to specify to what degrees the resource is not going to be available. Rows are going to be the smallest object in the whole database that you are able to work with when you are doing manipulations. But the rows are not the only object type that you are able to work with when you do manipulations. Options like extents, tables, indices, and pages can be as well. And you also have a chance to lock up the entire database if you need to.

Before we move on here, we need to take a look at a process that is known as an extent. This is basically going to be the physical allocation of data, and the database engine is going to employ this lock if a table or an index grows, and more space on the disk is needed to hold onto it.

These can be used in some cases, but problems will come up when you use some of the locks, including a deadlock or a lock escalation, and it is important to be on the lookout for one of these. Before you start using the locks, it is best if you can get a full understanding of how these locks and how they work in the database so that you are able to use them in the proper manner.

The final chapter that we are going to take a look at in this guidebook is going to discuss some of the SQL administration, but it is useful before we get to this point to mention that Oracle was able to develop a few extensions for SQL, and one of these allows for procedural instruction using the SQL syntax. This extension is going to be known as PL/SL, and as we discussed a bit earlier, SL all on its own is not able to provide some of the procedural instructions that we need because it is going to be a non-procedural language.

The extension that is listed above is going to help fix this problem because it is responsible for extending out some of the capabilities that come with the SQL language. The PLSQL code is going to be used in many different manners, but for the most part, it is going to be used to help create and modify some of the more advanced concepts of SQL, such as the functions, stored procedures, and triggers.

Triggers are going to make it so that SL is able to perform specific operations as long as the conditional instructions have been defined with it. This means that when you do this, you are working with more advanced functionality of SQL, and this will often work at the same time with logging or alerts to notify both the principles and the administrators, depending on how you have this all set up when there are some errors in the database.

Remember here that the basic SQL code is not going to have the right kinds of control structures to do things like decision making, branching, and looping, which may be available in some of the coding languages including

Java. Because of this, the PL/SQL was developed in order to meet the needs of the database product, which includes some of the functionality like the ones we talked about. Basically, this extension was developed to make sure that the SQL language was able to do some of the same functionalities that Java and other coding languages rely on as well. This ensures that you are able to get the most out of your SQL language when working in a database.

In addition, we also took a look at some of the topics of functions, we found that we talked a bit about functions that were user-defined, but we did not show how you were able to define them. This is another place where the SQL language does not adequately cover the creation of these kinds of functions. The good news is that when you use the right kind of program, you are able to create some functions that fit in well within the same scope as the system-defined functions that are accepted in SQL.

As a reminder, the user-defined function, or UDF, is going to be a construct of programming that is going to accept parameters, will perform tasks that can help the database use the parameters that the system defined, and will return the right results in a successful manner. These UDF's are going to be tricky in some cases because the SQL from Microsoft is going to allow for things that are known as stored procedures that are going to be able to accomplish the same task as these user-defined functions.

And finally, we need a quick word on the stored procedures. These are going to be a batch of statements in SQL that are going to be executed in more than one way, while also containing some centralized data access logic. Both of these features are going to be important when you work in SQL in production environments, but we won't go too much into this as it is above the beginner level for now.

Though we went into more details about some of the topics that we were able to talk about in this chapter, you will find that it helps to provide some great examples of how you are able to use SQL in the real world. There are so many companies and other entities that are going to rely on databases to help them keep track of the information that they need, whether this has to do with their employees or with their customers and even with their products.

There is a lot of information that a company is going to need to go through and keep track of overtime. And it is possible that they are going to have several different databases. The number of databases that a company has will depend on how big they are, but it is not uncommon to see them with a database for managing employees and employee work, one for customers, and one for any products that they end up selling.

Almost any company and industry will be able to work with these databases and see that it can benefit them. They can use it even if they provide more of a service to their customers rather than a lot of different products. But when you are storing information for your customers or for your employees, and you want to make sure that you are able to keep track of the products as well, then the topics we have been going through in this chapter, and with the rest of the guidebook, will be helpful for you.

There is so much that you can do when it comes to using a database in your business. And while there are many options to helping you get this database done, one of the best methods to go with is SQL. It is simple to use, doesn't take a lot of time to learn, and the coding is one of the easiest to learn out of all the programming languages.

Chapter 11: The Use of Database Administration

The last topic that we are going to look at here is the idea of database administration. Database administration, as well as database functionality, are going to be separate topics that all work on their own, but they are still very critical aspects that come with SL, and any base of knowledge is not going to be complete without having a chance to understand these related fields and how they relate to the SQL.

There are a lot of different administrative tasks that have to happen on a daily basis. Some of the most important ones that we need to talk about right now are going to include creating backups of the database the company is using, creating backups of the logs, and doing some performance management. In addition to this, there are going to be some other associated pieces of information that need to come into place including understanding how the storage of the database works, as well as the automation and the utilities of the database, but these are some areas of knowledge that will help them administrator become more effective, and won't really be involved in a direct manner in the maintenance of the database.

As we take a look at the SQL language, we can see that it contains some databases that are related to system information. These kinds of databases are going to provide some high-level information about the whole database system. This information is important because it is going to give the administrators at a glance data regarding the health and how well the performance of the database is doing.

The primary system database is what we are going to call the master database. Then when we look at the storage of the disk here, the basic unit for the storage is going to be known as "a page" or 8KB., and every database is only going to be one page in length, at least until the data contained inside of it is going to expand the database out to multiple pages. This can take some time depending on the size of your database and how quickly it ends up expanding out.

There are also going to be some utility functions that are going to exist inside of this language as well including bulk copy, which is going to allow the statements that you write out in this system to be entered into the command prompt.

Another part of administration on this language is going to be policy-based management. This will be based on the rules and the policies that are set up by a particular company and is customizable based on the company that is using it. This is basically a feature that is going to allow an administrator to control how the database is created and configured across all of the different user bases that are there. This is going to reinforce the data consistency, but can also make the job of the administrator a bit easier because they get to enforce the amount of consistency in how they maintain the database overall.

The database administrators, who are called DBA in SQL, will be responsible for creating the redundancy that is needed and to maximize the uptime on a database resource. They are able to do this because they assume and plan for the failure of the structures of the database. While no one wants the database to fail, they like to plan for this in case it does happen. The worst-case scenario with the database is that it would fail, but this is not something that the DBA should see as a possible outcome. This is going to cause a lot of problems with the system, could lose a lot of valuable information and this can cause more problems down the line.

Failure of the physical assets housing a database is a guarantee if enough time passes. The strain that can happen on the machine is high, and even under the steadiest of temperatures, there is a known limit on the number of re-writes that the physical dish is able to take on before the drive ends up failing. Redundancy is going to be created through housing data on some arrays that won't be able to come with data loss if you see that one of the nodes in the array fails. But there are other things that can cause failures in the system such as coding failures, power outages, and other things could cause some issues to the physical structure of that database if they are not taken care of in the proper manner.

The good news is that an experienced DBA is going to prepare and be ready in case any of these possibilities happen and most of them would be able to create some kind of solution that is automated so that, if failure happens (though they try to prevent it from ever happening), the least amount of data would be sacrificed as possible.

As our world of technology continues to grow and change, and we move more into the era of using cloud computing, the losses that are going to happen with failure will be pretty much nothing. But even when one of these companies doesn't decide to work with cloud computing, it is possible to do an automated backup of the database on a regular basis to make sure that the information is saved and ready to go.

If you are a DBA working with this kind of system, it is important to have something in place to handle the unexpected. You can prepare all that you want and try to avoid these problems as much as you can, but there is going to be times when things don't always go your way. Assuming that the worst is going to happen at any moment, and working with things like cloud computing if you can or at least having some backup that happens on a regular basis throughout the day, can ensure that if something happens the information from the database is saved and will do just fine when the system comes back up.

The next thing that we need to take a look at is how well the database is performing. This is something that the administration is going to need to deal with, but there are a lot of different factors that need to come into play with this one as well. Throughput and response times are the measurable that will help to quantify the performance. To start, the response time is going to measure a single operation from query to response, and throughput is able to help measure the overall ability to process transactions to the limit that the engine of the database is going to able to handle. There are three factors that we have to pay attention to if you are worried about the performance of the database, and these are going to include the available resources, the systems, and the database applications.

These three aspects are even able to be broken down into other things based on what you would like to look through and check out. This is because the system is going to have a lot of different parts. For example, when you are trying to work with the performance of your system, you need to look at things like how much memory is available, the speed of the CPU, the limitations on the system, the query optimization, and more. All of these factors are elaborated upon in previous chapters, which helps us to see more about what they are able to do and why they are so important to making this process work.

When we are looking at some of the more practice usages that come with this, the database system could contain a minimum of five hundred little databases, and each one is going to have their own coded statements, indices, and tables. The performance of the database is usually not going to be that big of a problem until the database has enough data that the speed of computing just isn't strong enough to override the efficiency.

This could be something that becomes a widespread situation in practice, and it is likely that many companies are going to rely on expert consultants to help deal with this kind of situation if it does arise in their company. This is because all of the offending factors are going to be so large in number, and in the case of doing SQL coding, it can be challenging to identify the full problem at hand.

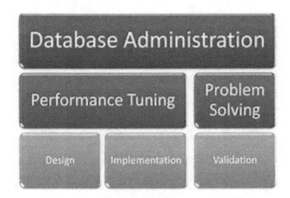

With a good DBA, these problems should not be such a big deal, and you will be able to prevent them from happening in the first place. But when the DBA does not have the right experience to handle what is going on in the code, and they are not sure of the steps that they need to take to maintain and protect the database, it could result in some issues in the coding. This is when a professional is going to come in and can really help to fix the problems and will get the code to work the way that you need.

It is important to make sure that a competent DBA, and even a team of these individuals, will help you to manage your database and get it to work the way that you would like. This is an added expense for your business for sure, but the efficiency and the benefits that come with this will make the program work so much better than before.

The right DBA will be able to use the coding that comes with SQL to create and modify any of the tables and databases that you would like. They could take the customers or the employees who are able to use the database, and give those roles, allowing or restricting their access based on their role with the company and what they are allowed to see. If the CEO wants access to the database, they would have more than someone who is just working on one of the many projects in the database, for example. A customer would be limited to just being able to access their own account, rather than the account of anyone else who is on the system. This is one of the responsibilities that the DBA would be in charge of setting and monitoring.

In addition to keeping the database running well and making sure that no errors were going to come up, the DBA would need to work on the security that comes with the database. Those who are using the database expect that their information is going to be kept safe all of the time, and it would put a lot of people at risk, and harm the reputation of the company if they were not able to keep this information safe and secure for their customers and employees. This is why a DBA would need to spend some time and work, ensuring that the database is secure from all threats, internal and external, at all times.

Having a good DBA is going to make a big difference in how well the SQL database is going to work. They will be able to handle a lot of the different topics that we have discussed in this guidebook and will make sure that the database runs well and does what it should, with the help of the SQL coding language behind them.

Conclusion

Thank for making it through to the end of *SQL Programming*, let's hope it was informative and able to provide you with all of the tools you need to achieve your goals whatever they may be.

The next step is to start implementing some of the SQL languages into your business. There may be some other databases that you can use, and they may work with a lot of the different coding that you would need to do to keep information set and ready to go, but none are going to be as effective and helpful for helping you to manage your business as the SQL language.

This guidebook is going to help us learn more about the SQL language and some of the different things that you are able to with this database. This can help you to manage the data that you have, make it easier to pull up when it is needed, and so much more! No wonder so many businesses are running to use this kind of database to help them get results.

When you are ready to learn more about the SQL language and how to make it work for your needs, make sure to check out this guidebook and learn the steps that you need to make this process work for you.

Finally, if you found this book useful in any way, a review on Amazon is always appreciated!

Python Programming

A Pragmatic Approach To Programming Python for Total Beginners

Introduction

Congratulations on purchasing *Python Programming* and thank you for doing so.

The following chapters will discuss what you need to know to get started writing the Python language. There are many different aspects of the Python code, and learning how to use all of it, and make it work for your needs can go a long way in the types of programs that you are able to write. Python coding is not meant to be difficult, it is designed to be used by beginners and advanced coders alike, so learning how to make your own codes with the Python language is going to be easier than you may think!

In this guidebook, we are going to take a look at many of the different things that you are able to do with the Python code. We will look at some of the basics to start, including why the Python language is so beneficial and so popular how to get this program set up on any computer and operating system that you want to use, and even some of the basics of most codes to help you get started with the compiler and more.

From there, we are going to move on to some of the special parts that you are able to work on when you are ready to write your codes. By the time we are done with this section, you will find that you can write some amazing codes, ones that make sure your program is up and running and ready to go. Some of the topics that we are going to look at in this chapter to help us get the best results with our coding and with learning how to use the different aspects of Python include exception handling, loops, decision control statements, the iterators, the generators, functions, variables, classes and more!

The main point of this guidebook is to help you go from a new coder, someone who may have never worked with any kind of coding in the past, who is ready to get started writing some of their own codes. If this is your goal, and you want to see how efficient and easy the Python code can be, make sure to check out this guidebook to help you get started.

Publications with the same subject flood the market and we appreciate you picked our book! Rest assured we strive to provide information in this book is as fun and informational. Have fun reading!

Chapter 1: What is Python and Why Is It So Popular?

Learning how to properly code can open up a lot of doors and opportunities for you. Some people like to learn how to code because they have a neat idea for a program or an app that you would like to use. Maybe you find that there is a better job and more that you can get if you learned a bit of coding and how to do this kind of work. A big promotion could be yours when you learn how to do this. Alternatively, maybe you just want to learn how to do this in order to impress your friends and family.

If you are exploring some of the options that are available when you pick out a coding language, you may want to consider going with Python. This is one of the most popular coding languages out there, mainly because it is available on any platform, and it is easy enough for beginners to learn, while still having all the power that your programs need.

The Python language is going to be a coding language that is designed for beginners and that better-versed in coding to write some of their own programs. It is open-sourced, which means that anyone is able to get it for their computer free of charge. And there is a dedicated group of developers who will work on updating and keeping the program working well, which can ensure that you are able to use it for all of your needs on a regular basis.

One concept to keep in your head here though is that, while the Python program is open source and free to use, there are some libraries and some extensions that are going to cost you. These work well with the Python program, and they are not a fraud. But with some of them, there was another company that developed a special program or special features, and they are selling this. If you want to have special features, you may need to pay. If you just want to use the basic functions that come with Python, which are usually plenty enough for most people, then you will be able to do it for free.

You will find that there are actually a lot of different benefits that you are able to get when you decide to work with the Python code. Some of the different benefits that you are able to get when you choose to write codes with the Python language include:

It is open-sourced. One thing that many people like about the Python code is that it is open-sourced. This means that even though someone is going through and working on the development and keeping it up to date, anyone is able to download it online and get all of the files that they need to go with it. Moreover, they are able to do this all for free. This means that if you already have a computer ready to go, you can get started with writing your own codes and working with the Python language, without having to pay for a thing.

It has a large library. We are going to spend quite a bit of time in this guidebook exploring some of the things that come with the Python library, and what you are able to enjoy while working on this kind of library. This is going to include the variables, the functions, the classes and objects, and many of the other things that you need to do while writing some of your own codes in this language.

The Python library, at least the standard version, is going to come with all of the things that you need to start writing your own codes, and it is free. However, if you want to do things that are a bit more technical, like machine learning, mathematics, graphs, and so on, there are other libraries that you will have to download at the same time. You can pick and choose whether these are important to you or not.

It is easy for beginners to use. As a beginner, you will find that the Python language is going to be one of the easiest languages for you to learn. Sure, you can learn any of the others and this is not meant to stop you from that. However, the beauty of this language is that it was designed to be easier, while still having a lot of power, for most beginners to use. If you have shied away from using some of the other coding languages because you didn't think they would work that well for you, or you were worried that they would be too hard, then you can rest easy knowing that the Python language is going to be easy to work with and any beginner can write their own codes in no time.

It has enough power for even advanced coders to work with While Python is often advertised as a language that is used by beginners because it is easy to read and the coding is not as complicated as with some of the other languages out there, don't let this fool you. Even coders who have been working with this for a long time, and who may have worked with a few other coding languages along the way have found a lot to enjoy when it comes to working with the Python code.

This is because the Python code is not just simple, it is also powerful. It is going to be able to keep up with a lot f the processing and a lot of the power that we see with some of the other coding languages but it is going to be easier to use, and it is written out in a way that makes it easier to read through as well. This is why this program is perfect for both beginners and those are more advanced coders to work with.

This coding language is also all about the classes and the objects. We will talk about this a bit more as we progress through this book, but this really makes coding easier for you. It ensures that when you call up a part of the code, as long as you name it and call it up in the right away, it is going to show up the way that you want. This may have been a struggle for some beginners in other coding languages, but this problem is solved with the help of the Python code.

It can work with other languages. Not only are you able to turn on the Python language and use all of the capabilities that come with it on your computer, but you can also combine it together with some other coding languages to really enhance some of the capabilities that you see on there. Python is able to do many different things, but there are a few points where it may fall a bit short, or that other coding languages are going to do better. Adding it together with one of these other coding languages can ensure that your program is written the way that you want.

Python is already being used in many different programs already. In fact, some of your favorite programs may already be using Python to help them run. You will find that Python is on many website and games and other common programs, and you may not have even noticed to begin. As we go through this guidebook, you may be pleasantly surprised at how great these programs work, even though many of the codes are simple to read and write.

It can be added to any computer. You will find that with some of the other coding languages out there, you will be limited based on the type of operating system that you use. This can be a pain because either you need to change up your operating system in order to use it, or you will not be capable to employ that coding language at all.

The neat thing about working in the Python language is that this is not a problem. You will not have to worry about what kind of operating system is already on your computer, and you will not be limited by the operating system at all, because Python is going to work on all of them. We will take a look at some of the different steps that you can take to make sure the Python files and program are ready to go on your computer.

There is a large community that you can work with. As you go through some of the coding that you want to work with, you may find that there is a part of the code that you are not sure about, an error that may come up, or you just need some help or another that you want to explore. If you were all on your own, this could be frustrating because you would be unsure of how to proceed.

The good news with this one is that the Python language is really popular throughout the world, which means that you will be able to find many other programmers, beginners and advanced, who will share their knowledge with you. You can ask questions, look at forums, or even watch some videos to learn what you need and to make sure that you will get the code written the way that you want.

There is just so much to love about the Python coding language. This guidebook is going to go over many of the different types of codes that you are able to write, and adding them together can ensure that you get the right code written for your needs, no matter what your goal for the end results are. Now that you know some of the benefits that come with this coding language, and how the Python language can work well with you, let's move on to installing the language, so we can really get some use out of writing our own codes!

Chapter 2: Setting Up the Python Program

Before we can start to work on some of the codes that you want to write with Python, we need to make sure that we are able to go through and actually download this program on our computer. You have to work with getting the files set up so that they work the right way, and unless you have certain versions of the Mac OS, you will need to install and download it first.

There are several places where you are able to get the Python program and make sure it is set up. One of the easiest to use though is www.python.org. This one is going to include all of the files that you need to make Python code writing work including the compiler, the interpreter, and the IDLE. You can choose to get the download from somewhere else if you would like, but double-check whether they have all three of the options above, or if you need to download some of your own before starting.

Python is able to work on any operating system that you want to use it with. With that in mind though, each type of operating system is going to have slightly different rules that you need to follow to get the system set up and ready to go. Some of the steps that you can take to get the Python program installed on any computer system that you would like.

Installing Python on Windows

The first operating system that we are going to look at here is the Windows system. This is a popular one for many programmers to use, but since it has its own coding language on it already, you will have to manually go through and install it on your system if you want to use Python. This one may take a few steps, but most of them are really easy and you can really get the Python code on your computer and working well in a few minutes once you get the hang of what you are doing.

Python is going to be just fine and will work the way that you want when you put it on a Windows computer. It is just not, there to start with because of Windows has its own coding program. All this means is that you need to take the steps to install it on your system to get it set up. Nevertheless, once you go through the installation steps that we will talk about in a minute, you will be able to enjoy the power and the ease of the Python language, even when you are on a Windows computer.

When you are ready to work with the Python language on your computer that has the Windows operating system, you will need to start out by going through and coming up with the right variables for the environment, so that you can actually run the scripts for Python from the command prompt that is there. The rest of the steps that you can follow to make sure that Python works well for your needs includes:

1. To help us get started with setting all of this up, go to the Python download page on their website and grab the installer that is listed for the Windows operating system. You can choose to go with any version of Python that you like but most coders like to work with the latest version of Python 3. The installer is going to give you the 32-bit version of Python, but you can change that based on the version of the operating system you are using with Windows.

2. Once you have the Windows installer from the Python website, it is time to right-click on it and select "Run as Administrator". As you do this, the system is going to provide you with two options that you need to decide on. For this, click on "Customize Installation."

3. On the screen that comes up next, make sure that all of the boxes that are under "Optional Features" have been selected and then click to go to the next page.

4. While you are still under the "Advanced Options", you will need to pick out the location where you would like to install Python. Once that folder is picked out, you can click to install. This takes a bit of time to install so have some patience with it. Once that install is done, you can close out of this part.

5. The next thing that we need to do is set up the PATH variable that works with this system so that you have all of the directories that will include packages and other components that are necessary to use later on. The way that you get all of this set up is going to use the steps below;

a. Open up your Control Panel. If you are not certain where this is, click on your taskbar and type in "Control Panel". Click on the little icon that shows up when you do this.

b. When you get the Control Panel to show up, you can check for "Environment" and then click on Edit the System Environment Variables. When this is done, you can then click on the button tagged "Environment Variables."

c. At this point, you can go to the section that is listed for User Variables. Either here you can decide to create a new PATH variable, or you can edit the PATH variable that is already in place.

d. If there is not a variable for PATH on the system as you are looking, then it is time for you to create your own. To do this, click on New. Give it a name, one that works for the PATH variable you are choosing, and then place it into the chosen directory. Click to closer yourself from the Control Panel at this time and then go to the next step.

6. When you get to this point, you can open up that Command Prompt again. You can do this by clicking on your Start Menu, then clicking on Windows System, and finally on Command Prompt. Type in the word "python". This will be enough to load up the interpreter of Python for you. \

Once you have been able to go through the steps above, which are actually faster than they may seem at the time, you will then be able to open up the Python language and use it in any manner that you would like in the Windows system.

You can even choose to get the interpreter and other parts of this code set up the way that you want them to and then write out codes when you are ready for that step.

Installing Python with the Linux operating system

The second type of operating system that you are able to work with is known as the Linux operating system, and this works well with the Python language as well. This operating system is really taking off, and it is able to work with a ton of different programs and systems that some of the others are not always able to handle. This makes it perfect for doing some of the coding that you want with the Python language, which is why we are going to take some time to explore how to download Python on this system.

The first thing to do here is to see if there is a variant of Python 3 is on your system. You can open up the command prompt on Linux and then run the following code:

$ python3 - - version

If you are on Ubuntu 16.10 or newer, then it is a simple process to install Python 3.6. You just need to use the following commands:

$ sudo apt-get update

```
$ sudo apt-get install Python3.6
```

If you are relying on an older version of Ubuntu or another version, then you may want to work with the deadsnakes PPA, or another tool, to help you download the Python 3.6 version. The code that you need to do this includes:

```
$ sudo apt-get install software-properties-common
$ sudo add-apt repository ppa:deadsnakes/ppa
# suoda apt-get update
$ sudo apt-get install python3.6
```

The good news that you are going to enjoy with this one is that if you choose to work with some of the other distributions that happen to come in the Linux family, it is possible that these systems already have Python 3 on them. It is all going to depend on the distribution that you use and whether they upgraded to have this or not.

If you find that this does not have the Python 3 on it as you would like or if the version of Python is not the one that you would like, you will just need to use the steps above in order to install the version of Python that you would like. Linux makes it pretty easy to work with Python and to get it all set up so you can start to write some of your own codes in no time.

Installing with the Mac OS X

The next option that we are going to focus on to make sure that we get the Python language installed on our computer is how to get it to work with the Mac operating system. It is likely that the Python 2 program is going to already be on this kind of operating system, so if you see that this is there, then there is not any more to do. Python 2 is just fine to work with and can help you to get things done. However, some people prefer to code with a more recent version of python rather than this one and will choose to work with one of the Python 3 options.

If you just want to check out which version of Python is on your computer, then you can open up your command prompt and type in "python – V". You will see the name of which version of Python 2 is there, and then you can choose if this is the one that you want or not.

If the Python 2 version is not up to date like you want, or you want to change to Python 3, which is possible as well with the Mac operating system, it is just going to take a few more steps to make this happen. Before we go through all of those steps though, we need to double-check whether Python 3 is present on the computer so you do not waste time. To do this, type in "python3 – V" and see if this gives you any results.

If you are not able to get results from this, and you want to get the Python 3 program set up on your Mac computer, make sure that you first uninstall the Python 2 version so that you do not get any confusion on the system. When that is off the computer, visit www.python.org as we discussed before and then pick out the version of Python that you would like to add to your computer.

Being able to run both the shell and the IDLE with the Python language is going to depend on which version of the program you decide to work with, as well as what preferences are there when you write out the code. The two biggest commands that you are going to use the most often to help make sure that the shell and IDLE applications start-up when you want will vary based on the version you use, and they are:

- For Python 2.X just type in "Idle"
- For Python 3.X, just type in "idle3"

As we talked about a bit before, when you take the time to download and install this Python 3 on the Mac operating system, you will need to install the IDLE so make sure that is there, and you can install it as a standard application inside of your Applications folder of course. To help you to start up this program using your desktop, you just need to go into the folder, double click on the application for the IDLE, and then you can wait for it to download.

Chapter 3: Some of the Basic Parts of the Python Code

Now that we have had some time to explore what the Python language is all about and some of the benefits that come with it, and we have an exceptional idea of some of the distinct means that you can install this language on your computer to use it, it is now time to learn more about the Python code. We are going to really take a look at some of the basic components that tend to show up with Python, and how you will be able to implement these into your code, especially with some of the more complicated ones that we will discuss later on in this guidebook.

There are so many types of codes that you are able to work with when it comes to Python, and it is all going to depend on the kind of program that you want to write out as well. Making sure that you know these basic parts though, and gaining a good understanding of how they work will make it easier for you to really write some of those more complicated codes later on. So, let us get started on some of the basics that come with the Python code.

Working on those keywords

The first basic part that we are going to explore when it comes with the Python code is the keywords. All coding languages are going to have keywords that they reserve to tell the compiler which action it should take. These are seen as special because they will be the commands that the compiler needs to follow along the way. Using them in the wrong way or in the wrong part of the code can result in the code not giving you the results that you want.

As you are working with the keywords with this kind of language, you must make sure that you are using them properly. You do not want to add them to the wrong part of the code. This often leads to an error message and can make things a bit tricky to work with. As you work with this code a bit more, you will learn what words are seen as keywords, and which ones you should only use for this, to get the best results.

These keywords are responsible for one thing, and that is to provide the compiler with the commands that it needs and helps the compiler know what it is supposed to do when you execute that command. These keywords are important to all of the codes that you decide to do, so when you are working on some Python code, double-check that you always put the keywords in the right place for your needs.

Naming your identifiers

We need to take a moment to take a look at some of the steps that you need to follow in order to properly name some of the identifiers that show up in your code. If you are not able to name these properly, you are going to find a lot of frustration with writing out some codes in this language. So, now we need to take a look at what these identifiers are all about and why they are important in your code.

As you work through Python, you may find that there are quite a few different identifiers that you can work with, even though they come under many different names including variables, entities, functions, and classes. Any time that you would like to name one of these identifiers though, be happy and relieved to know that the rules for doing so will be the same and will apply to all of them. Once we go through the rules for naming that are below, you will be able to name any identifier that you would like.

This brings us to the idea of naming the identifiers and learning which rules you have to follow to make this happen. First, you need to take some caution concerning the name that you give to the identifier. There are a ton of names that are available, and you can choose, for the most part, the name that you want. You get the choice of working with letters, both the uppercase and the lower case, and any number. The underscore symbol and any combination of the previous will work as well.

But there are a few restrictions to keep in mind with this as well when you start naming your identifier. First, it is not allowed for you to name any identifier with a number, and the name should not have any spaces that come with it. Naming the identifier, something like 5kids or 5 kids would get you an error, but naming it five kids or five kids would be just fine. Moreover, keep in mind that you should never use a keyword as the name of one of your identifiers or the compiler is going to get confused.

When you come up with the name that you want to give to that identifier, make sure that you remember what it is. It may follow all of the rules that you need, but if you are not able to remember the name when it is time to execute the code or pull out that identifier later on, then there can be some issues. If you call it the wrong thing or you spell it differently, then there could be an error or the compiler is going to get confused.

With that in mind, if you pick a name that makes sense for the identifier that you are working with, and you make sure to follow the rules that you talked about above, then you are going to be just fine and the code will work the way that you would like.

Looking at the control flow

The control flow in this language can be important. This control flow is there to ensure that you wrote out the code the proper way. There are some types of strings in your code that you may want to write out so that the compiler can read them the right way. But if you write out the string in the wrong manner, you are going to end up with errors in the system. We will take a look at many codes int his guidebook that follows the right control flow for this language, which can make it easier to know what you need to get done and how you can write out codes in this language.

A word about statements

The next thing that we need to explore on our list is known as the statements. Statements are just sentences that show up in Python that you would like to have on the screen when the code executes. They are just strings of code that you will write out, and that you tell the compiler to list out on the screen. When you tell the compiler the instructions that you want it to be able to work on, you will find that those are going to be some of the statements in your code.

When it comes to the statements, as long as you are able to write them out in the proper manner, the compiler will be able to read them and will ensure that you get the message that you want to show up on the screen. Remember that you can make these statements either long or short, depending on what works for the code that you will work on. You will see many statements that show up in the codes that you write, including some of the examples that we list out in this guidebook.

Comments and how they work

Comments are another part of the code that you need to learn, and it is likely that you will see quite a few of these, especially at the beginning of any code that we decide to work with. There are going to be some times when you are writing out code inside of this language, and it seems like it is a favorable idea to include a note or some kind of explanation about what is happening in the code. You are able to do this with the help of a comment.

These comments can be nice because you can add them in so that someone reading through the code knows what is going on, but you will not see any effect with your program. It keeps things organized; helps to explain some of the things that you have going on in the code, and can make things easier, without any issues to how well your code is working.

As a programmer, you will see that it can be easy to add in these comments, and you can add in as many as you would like. To make your own comment in Python, you just need to add in "#" and then follow it with the statement that you want to have there. This sign is enough to tell the compiler that you are creating your own comment, and the compiler will see it, and avoid working on the comment at all, automatically skipping to the next part of the code.

You get the choice to add as many of these comments as you would like to the codes that you decide, as long as they are not just there to take up room and actually explain what is going to in that part of the code. You could have lines and lines of code if you would like, though most coders try to avoid this to keep the program working smoothly and to make it easier to read through any code that they write. But technically, as long as you have that symbol in front of your statement, it is possible to add in as many of these comments as you would like, and the compiler will know that it should not read that and should go to the next part of the code.

The variables

We also need to take a moment to talk about variables and how they are an important part of the Python code you are writing. They are going to be more common than you may originally think. The main reason that we need to take a look at the variables is that they are responsible for storing different values that you place inside of your code, and will make sure that any line of code that you decide to write is going to be organized, easy to read and will execute the way that you would like.

The best part is that they are simple to work with. All that you need to do in order to make sure that a value is correctly assigned to a variable is to add in an equal sign between the value and the variable, and the compiler will be able to do the rest for you. You can choose any value to go with your variable, just make sure that the equal sign is in place.

Another thing that is possible to do with the help of the variable is assigned more than one value to each variable. If you just add in the equal sign on both of these values and get them to go back to the variables you want to work with. If you take a look down at some of the different codes that we have written out and examples that are in this guidebook, you will find that there are many variables in place with them.

Ending with the operators

The final basic part of the Python code that we are going to take a look at here is known as the operators. These are going to be simple, and there are a lot of different operators out there that you are able to work with based on what kind of code. You can work with some that help you to add a few parts of your code together. You can work with some that will help you to assign names to your identifiers as we talked about before, and some that help to decide if a part of the code is considered true or false. Think of all the possibilities that you can do with these operators once you learn how to use them properly?

As you take a look through some of the different codes that we will work on in this guidebook, many different operators are going to show up. Moreover, often you will use them without even realizing what you are doing at the time or realizing that you are working with the operators. But it would be almost impossible to do any kind of coding if you were not able to add in the operators along with some of the other parts.

These are just a few of the basic parts that you are able to work on when it comes to creating your own codes in Python. These may seem simple, and you may wonder why you would need to use these in the first place, but there are so many times that you are going to see these basics show up in the code that you are trying to write, and having a strong working knowledge of them can make coding in Python so much easier.

Chapter 4: What are the Variables in Python?

The first topic that we are going to take a look at is the Python variables. We looked at this a bit before, but we need to go into more detail to see exactly why these variables are so important, and why they are going to help our code to work the way that we want. These variables are basically going to be anything that is able to hold a value, a value that is able to change. To keep it simple, the variable is just going to be a box that is able to hold onto things in the code. This is important because they will be able to pull out a saved space that is in your memory on the computer so that you are able to pull it out and use it in the code as needed.

These variables are going to be good for us to learn because you can store them into the memory of the code, and you are able to ask the compiler to pull these out when they are needed. This means that the variables that you decide to create are going to be placed throughout the memory, where there is room, on your computer, and if they are assigned properly, you will be able to find the variables that you need at the right time. Hinged on the type of data that you are aiming to do with, the variable is going to help the compiler know where to store the information so you can find it later.

Now that we have some idea of how the variables are going to work, and some of the importance that comes with it, let us look at how to assign values to the variables, and some more of the neat things that we are able to do when it comes to the variables in the Python code.

How to assign a value to the variable

To make sure that we are able to get our variable to act the way that we want, it is important to assign at least one value over to the variable. Without a value, and if you miss this step, then you will end up saving something in the memory like normal, but space is going to be empty, and when the compiler does its work, it won't pull up anything when the code runes. If the variable is taken care of the way that it should, and you assign a value to it, and sometimes even more than one value to the same variable, then the memory will have something saved in that spot and the code will work properly.

As we go through and work on these variables, you are going to find that the process is going to include three options that are available to work with. Each of these can be useful, and the method that you pick often depends on what you want to have happened inside the code. The three types of variables that you are going to be able to pick out from include:

- Float: this would include numbers like 3.14 and so on.
- String: this is going to be like a statement where you could write out something like "Thank you for visiting my page!" or another similar phrase.

- Whole number: this would be any of the other numbers that you would use that do not have a decimal point.

When you are working with variables in your code, you need to remember that you do not need to take the time to make a declaration to save up this spot in the memory. This is automatically going to happen once you assign a rate over to the variable using the match a sign. If you want to check that this is going to happen, just look to see that you added that equal sign in and everything is going to work.

Assigning a value over to your variable is pretty easy. Some examples of how you can do this in your code would include the following:

x = 12   *#this is an example of an integer assignment*

pi = 3.14   *#this is an example of a floating point assignment*

customer name = John Doe   *#this is an example of a string assignment*

This is just part of the equation and only one of the options that you are able to do with this. We also mentioned for a bit in this chapter how it is possible to assign two or more values to the same variable if you would like. This may not happen as often as you would see with just having one variable to one value, but there may be certain instances in your code where you will need to make sure that two values are stored in the same place in the computer memory, and so you will assign these two values to the same variable.

This means that we need to learn how to make this happen. To assign two values to the same variable, you will need to work with pretty much the same steps that we talked about above. You just need to make sure that there are equal signs between each value that attaches them back to the variable that you are working on as well. It is as simple as that.

Let us take a look at how to make this happen. A good example would be something like a = b = c = 1 to show the compiler that all three of those values are going to go back to the variables. You can also choose to work with something like 1 = b = 2 to show that there are two values that go with that particular variable. You can choose which of these two methods works best for what you want to do there.

The one thing that we need to remember when it comes to doing with these variables is that it needs to be given a value. A variable without a value is going to be worthless as it means nothing will happen at that point in the code. When this is done, and the variable has at least one value that has been attached back to it, you know that the piece of memory that the variable is holding has been filled and that the compiler will know how to call back the value when the program is up and running.

Chapter 5: Working with Functions

Now that we have had a chance to learn about the variables and how they store some values in the memory of the computer for us, it is now time to look a bit more at some other topics that are going to help us get more done in this code. For this part, we are going to take a look at functions, because this is something that will be mentioned quite a bit through this guidebook. Let us dive right into the functions and learn how to make these works in the proper manner inside our Python code.

To start out this topic, we are going to look at the functions and what they are all about. These functions are going to be known for being a set of expressions, which is sometimes called the statements as well. These can come in two main methods either with a name, or they are going to be kept anonymous based on how you want to use them. They are going to be some of the first-class objects that you add into the code, which means that there won't already be a lot of restrictions on how you are able to use them in your code.

With these functions, you will find that you can use them in a similar manner that values in the code are used, even like the strings and the numbers, and they will have some attributes that we need to lookout. You can bring out the attributes using the dir prefix in the code.

Functions are special because they can be very diversified, and they will show up in many different parts of the code that you are writing. Moreover, they are going to bring in many attributes that you are able to bring into the code as you create the functions. A few of the choices that are available to use when you create some of these functions include:

- __doc__: This is going to return the docstring of the function that you are requesting.
- Func_default: This one is going to return a tuple of the values of your default argument.
- Func_globals: This one will return a reference that points to the dictionary holding the global variables for that function.
- Func_dict: This one is responsible for returning the namespace that will support the attributes for all your arbitrary functions.
- Func_closure: This will return to you a tuple of all the cells that hold the restrained for the complimentary variables inside of the function.

There are different things that you can do with your functions, such as passing it as an argument over to one of your other functions if you need. Any function that is able to take on a new one as the argument will be considered the higher-order function in the code. These are good to learn because they are important to your code as you move.

Chapter 6: Exception Handling in Python

There are many cool things that you are able to do when you work on the Python coding language. Some of them are going to be relatively simple and will help you to just write out some simple statements on the screen, and others are going to take it a bit farther and try to write out full codes and more, and even games and other programs while you use many different techniques.

With this in mind, we are going to move on to a look at exception handling with the help of Python. As you start to create some of the codes that you would like to work on in Python, you are going to find that there are some exceptions that can show up. Sometimes these are exceptions that the program is going to automatically recognize and will bring up for you, and other times you will be able to create on your own in order to make a particular program work. Any of them that the code ends up showing to you automatically are going to be found in the Python library, so you can go ahead and peruse that if you are interested in learning more.

For example, let us say that the user gets to a certain part of your code and they want to start dividing by zero. This is something that the Python language, as well as many of the other coding languages out there, are not going to allow to happen. We will look at how this exception is going to look in the code, as well as some of the things that you can do to change up the exception and make sure that it makes sense and actually goes along with your code.

In addition to some of the automatic exceptions that your code is going to start bringing up for you, it is possible that you can raise some of your own. This is going to depend on the kind of code that you are trying to write. If there is something within the program that you would like to limit, or you want to make sure that the user is not able to do something, then this is when you would want to add in the exception.

Now, we need to focus on the automatic exceptions, the ones that the program already recognizes on its own. If the user end sup doing one of these things that the program will not allow, the exception will be raised and the program is not going to let it all finish. This could be something like calling up the wrong name of a function, dividing by zero, and so on.

As a programmer, it is important that you have a good idea of some of the different exceptions that are going to show up in your code, and looking through the Python library is going to help you with this. This helps you to know how to write out each part of the code and can help you be prepared for what can turn up in the code as well. A few of the most common exceptions that are going to show up in the Python code, along with some of their keywords, will include the following:

1. Finally: This is going to be the action that you want to put in because it helps to do any cleanup actions that need to be done in the code, whether the exception is brought up in this particular code or not.

2. Assert: This is a condition that will make sure that the exception is triggered inside of the code.

3. Raise: This raise command is a good one to learn about because it is going to help you to manually get an exception raised inside of your code if you want to create your own.

4. Try or except: This option is going to be when you want to be able to see whether a block of code is going to work, and then that code is recovered thanks to the exceptions. The exceptions that save the code can either by ones that you raise or by ones that the Python code automatically raises for you.

How to raise these exceptions in your code:

The first thing that we need to take a look at here is the idea of how you would be able to use these exceptions that can come up in your code, especially when they are automatic exceptions. When these exceptions end up in your code, it is important for you as the programmer to be prepared and to know what you are able to do with some of the codings in order to get past them and to make them even easier to understand.

Let us say that you are designing your own code, and you notice that there is a place where the user could potentially have an exception show up. You can then take a look at any notice that the compiler is going to bring up when you use the code, and see if it is raising this kind of exception. This shows up because your program has had a chance to look through the code, it seems that this problem is there, and now it wants to know what you would like to have done.

The good news here is that often, the issues that raise the exceptions that are automatic are pretty easy for you to fix. For example, you or the user may try to bring up a file, and it was either given the wrong name or when you went to search for it, you typed in the wrong name. The compiler is not going to be able to find a match when you do this, and that is when it raises an exception. The program was able to look through the code and sees that there is nothing it can do to help.

Now, this can seem like a complicated process to work within your code, but it does have many benefits. A good way to start to see how these exceptions are going to work is to take some time and make our own example. We can then see what will happen with our compiler, and how it can raise an exception when we set it all up. An example of a code that you can type into the compiler to make this happen includes:

x = 10

y = 10

```
result = x/y #trying to divide by zero

print(result)
```

The output that you are going to get when you try to get the interpreter to go through this code would be:

```
>>>
Traceback (most recent call last):
    File "D: \Python34\tt.py", line 3, in <module>
    result = x/y
ZeroDivisionError: division by zero
>>>
```

When you have had some time to put this example into your compiler, you will see that there is an error or an exception is raised, because the user has gone through the code and is trying to divide by zero, which is not allowed with this kind of coding.

As a programmer, you have a choice now. You can definitely just leave the code like this and get the error message above. However, when your user comes on, looks at this, and sees that long and messy error message, how likely is it that they will have any idea what is going on? They will probably not understand what is going on, and it will just look like a mess to them. This is why we need to take this a step further and work on creating a code that is easier to read and to change up the message that comes up when you do the exception handling.

A better idea is to look at some of the different options that you can add to your code to help prevent some of the mess from before. You want to make sure that the user understands why this exception is being raised, rather than leaving them confused in the process. A different way that you can write out this code to make sure that everyone is on the same page includes:

```
x = 10
y = 0
result = 0
try:
        result = x/y
        print(result)
except ZeroDivisionError:
        print("You are trying to divide by zero.")
```

If you take some time to type this into the compiler and then compare to the answer that we got above, you will find that the error message that shows up is going to be a lot easier to read, and the user will actually understand what they did wrong. They can look at this message, and then go back through and make the changes that are needed. You do not have to add in this, but when it comes to making an easily usable code, it is a nice addition to have.

Defining an exception that is all your own.

In the work that we did above, we were able to see how to handle some of the exceptions that are going to come up because they are found in the Python library. This is a good way to gain some familiarity with the idea of exceptions and will help you to change it up and make the messages easier to work with if you would like, rather than leaving it as a string of numbers and letters that you will struggle with, much less your user.

Now we need to take it to the next level and look at how you are able to take something that would normally be fine in the code, and turn it into an exception. This can be done in a lot of games that you would like to make, or a few other examples where you want to limit what the user is able to do at that particular time.

Maybe you decide to work on some kind of code and you want to make sure that only certain letters or certain numbers, or a certain number of times that they can try something out at this point. Often games or forms are going to need to use this to its advantage. The way that you raise an exception is going to depend on the kind of programming that you are trying to create, but the same basic ideas are going to apply.

When you do these kinds of exceptions, you will find that they are going to be really unique to the type of code that you are writing. If you did not add in the right coding for this, then the compiler will not recognize that there is a problem, and it will continue to run the program the way that it wants, rather than the way that you want it designed. The neat thing here is that you are able to add in any kind of exception that you would like here and write out any message, and it is going to follow an idea that is similar to what we did in the other section.

Let us break this down a bit and look at some of the steps that you can take in order to really write out your own exceptions, along with the messages that go with them, in the code you are doing:

```
class CustomException(Exception):
def_init_(self, value):
        self.parameter = value
def_str_(self):
        return repr(self.parameter)


try:
        raise CustomException("This is a CustomError!")
except CustomException as ex:
        print("Caught:", ex.parameter)
```

When you finish this particular code, you are done successfully adding in your own exception. When someone does raise this exception, the message "Caught: This is a CustomError!" will come up on the screen. You can always change the message to show whatever you would like, but this was there as a placeholder to show what we are doing. Take a moment here to add this to the compiler and see what happens.

Exception handling is something that you will work with a lot more as you start to write out some more advanced codes in Python. There are a lot of times that you will work either with the exceptions that are recognized by the program or ones that you want to bring up for the code that you are writing in particular. Working with some of the codes that we bring up in this chapter will help you to deal with these exceptions and will ensure that you are able to make them look good to the user. Make sure to try a few of these codes in your compiler to ensure that you get some practice with these exceptions and that you are able to get a good idea of how these exceptions are supposed to work.

Chapter 7: The Elif or Conditional Statements

While it would be nice to set, up a program and get it to behave in the manner that we want all of the time. We would love to be able to guess all of the answers that someone is going to give us when they use the program, but in many cases, this is going to be impossible. For example, if you have a code that asks the user what their favorite color is, it is going to take forever to write out a code that has all of the colors of the world, and it is likely that you would miss some. Plus, that would take a long time and make the code look messy.

When you want to write out a code that is able to make decisions for you, based on some of the conditions that you set, then it is time to bring in the conditional statements, also known as the decision control statements. Pretty much any time that you are going to allow the user to add in an answer on their own, rather than listing out a menu with options for them, you will need to use these decision control statements so that the computer starts to know what steps you want it to take based on your conditions.

The first thing that we need to take a look at is the fact that there are going to be three different types of conditional statements. These include the if statement, the if else statement, and the elif statement. We will take a look at each of these to learn how they work, and when you may want to use them to make your code work properly.

The first of the conditional statements we are going to take a look at is known as the if statement. This one is pretty simple, and there may not be a ton of chances to use it in your code. But it still does work in the code, and can be a great way to learn more about these conditional statements.

The if the statement is going to rely on the idea that the answer the user gives is either true or false. The answer matches up with the conditions that you set, or it does not. This does not mean that the answer the user gives is wrong. It just means that it does not match up with the conditions that you have set up there at all and that is how the computer sees it. If the user puts in an answer that the computer agrees with, then they are going to get the information that you added into the code. But if the compiler sees the answer and determines it is false, then the program is going to end because it simply doesn't really know what it is supposed to do next (unless you added in more to handle this).

To get a better idea of how the if the statement is going to look, and how it is able to work, inside of your code, take a look at an example of the if statement that we have below:

```
age = int(input("Enter your age:"))
if (age <=18):
        print("You are not eligible for voting, try next election!")
print("Program ends")
```

Let us explore what is going to happen with this code when you put it into your program. If the user comes to the program and puts that they are younger than 18, then there will be a message that shows up on the screen. In this case, the message is going to say "You are not eligible for voting, try next election!" Then the program, as it is, is going to end. However, what will happen to this code if the user puts in some age that is 18 or above?

With the if statement, nothing will happen if the user says that their age is above 18. The if statement just has one option and will focus on whether the answer that the user provides is going to match up with the conditions that you set with your code. The user has to put in that they are under the age of 18 with the if statement in this situation or you will not be adept to get the program to happen again.

As you can imagine when you are working on this, there could be a few problems that arise when you try to use them if statement in some of the codes that you write. Your goal with the example above is not to force the user to put in a certain age to make the program work. You want them to put in any age that they actually are at the time. Their age is not wrong, and it is not true or false, so there are some limitations to what you are able to do with the if statements. This is why the if-else statements, as well as the elif statements that we will talk about in a minute, are going to be important to work with as well.

First, we are going to look at the if-else statements. These are going to follow the same kind of idea as we find with the if statements above, but it helps to solve some of the problems that you may encounter, and will make it easier to get the right response based on the input from the user. This statement is going to help your user to get an answer, no matter what age group they decide to put into the program.

Going from the idea that we talked about above, you will want to allow the user to come in and input any age that they want into the system. When you use the if-else statement, you can separate the ages based on those who are under 18, and those who are 18 and above, and then have responses show up in the program for each one. Let us peek at an instance that shows us how these if-else statements are going to work:

age = int(input("Enter your age:"))
if (age <=18):

        print("You are not eligible for voting, try next election!")
else

        print("Congratulations! You are eligible to vote. Check out your local polling station to find out more information!)
print("Program ends")

As you can see, this really helps to add some more options to your code and will ensure that you get an answer no matter what results the user gives to you. You can also change up the message to say anything that you want, but the same idea will be used no matter the answer that the user gives.

You have the option to add in some more possibilities to this. You are not limited to just two options as we have above. If this works for your program, that is just fine to use. However, if you need to use more than these two options, you can expand out this as well. For example, take the option above and expand it to have several different age groups. Maybe you want to have different options come for those who are under 18, those that are between the ages of 18 and 30, and those who are over the age of 30. You can separate it out in that way and when the program gets the answer from the user, it will execute the part that you want.

You are not limited to this one though. There are many examples of how the if-else statement is going to be able to add in some strength to the types of programs you are writing. Let us say that you wish to write out a program that allows the user to pick out the color that is their favorite. You may go through the program and list out six colors with responses to it. The user may pick one of those six colors, or they may pick something completely different.

If the user picks out a color that is on your list, then they are going to get the statement or the result that you have listed with it. However, if they pick out a different color that is on the list (which is possible because it would be very hard to list out all of the colors in the world), then the catchall or the final message is going to show up.

This catch-all, or the "else" part of the code, is something that is so important and you need to make sure to add it into this code if you are working with an if-else statement. In many cases of using these conditional statements, it is going to be impossible to think up all of the answers that someone is going to put in, and this can take forever even if you try. The catch-all part of this is going to catch any answer that is put in and does not match with the ones that you have listed out earlier in the code.

The if-else statement is a great one to learn how to use because it helps you to handle a situation where the user is going to have many different potential answers, and you want to make sure you get a response for all of them. If you do not have a statement to handle any of the cases you missed with answers from the user, then the else part of the statement will handle it for you and can make the code run smoothly.

Now that we have had a chance to work with the if statement and with the if-else statement, it is time to move on to what is known as the elif statements. This is going to take the ideas that we have been talking about with the other two conditional statements and bring it a bit further. This one is also going to follow the idea of a menu option. The user will be given a menu of what they want to pick from, and then when they make a choice, your program will execute the kind of statement that you want.

There are many codes that are going to utilize the elif statement, and it just depends on what you are trying to write. One good example of when you are going to see the elif statement is during a game when a menu style of choices comes up and you have to make a decision based on that information. These statements are going to be used if you want to provide more options than one or two back over to your user.

With the elif statement, you do have some freedom. You can choose to have as many of these statements present in the code as you want, as long as you write out the code in the proper manner and you make sure that you add in the right function to go along with them. In addition, having too many of these could mean that you have a complicated code that is a bit harder to write out than others, but if it works well for your program, then it is just fine to add in as many as you would like.

To better, understand how these elif statements are going to work, here is a good example of the syntax that comes with these statements:

if expression1:

statement(s)

elif expression2:

statement(s)

elif expression3:

statement(s)

else:

statement(s)

The above is going to just contain the syntax that you will need to use when you want to create your own elif statement in your code. You are able to add onto this or take away based on how many options you would like to provide to your user. Just take the syntax then, and add in the information that should go with each part.

As you get a chance to read through this syntax and see what is there, notice that there is a nice else statement that comes at the end, similar to what we saw with the if-else statement before. Just like before, you need to make sure that this is added into the code at the very end. It is critical to put that in so that it is able to get all of the answers that the user wants that do not fit with the options you list above.

What we looked at above is just the syntax that comes with the elif statements, but there is so much that you are able to do with this. Now that we have a better idea of how the syntax for the elif statement is supposed to look, let's go through and add in an example to see what it would look like, or similar to, when you use it inside of your own code:

Print("Let's enjoy a Pizza! Ok, let's go inside Pizzahut!")
print("Waiter, Please select Pizza of your choice from the menu")

```
pizzachoice = int(input("Please enter your choice of Pizza:"))
if pizzachoice == 1:
        print('I want to enjoy a pizza napoletana')
elif pizzachoice == 2:
        print('I want to enjoy a pizza rustica')
elif pizzachoice == 3:
        print('I want to enjoy a pizza capricciosa')
else:
        print("Sorry, I do not want any of the listed pizza's; please bring a Coca
Cola for me.")
```

Now the user is going to be able to go through and make the choices that they want and they will get the right option to meet with them. For example, if they want to go with the pizza rustica, they will pick the number 2. If they want to have, just a drink rather than one of the other choices above, they can do that too. While we did use the example of pizza in here, there are many other things that you can do with it, so pretty much if you want your user to have some options, you would use the syntax that is above and then fills in the options that work the best for you.

As we took some time to discuss in this guidebook, working with the conditional statements can add in a lot of great power to the codes that you are trying to write. The reason for this is that they do add in some more power than a few of the other options that we have talked about so far in this guidebook, helps the program to make decisions on its own, and can really change the game when working on your own codes.

To make sure that you get a good understanding of how to work with the conditional statements, all three of them, make sure to open up your compiler and add some of the codes into it. This gives you some practice with writing these and ensures that you can see how each one is similar and how each one is different.

Chapter 8: What are Loops and How Can They Help My Code?

There are many different things that you are able to do when it comes to working with the Python language. In addition, the next thing that we are going to explore and learn how to use are the loops. These loops are very important when you are writing your code and the amount of time that you are able to save when using it is going to make things so much easier in the long run. Loops help to clean up the program and can fit a lot of information in just a few lines of code, helping to make your life easier.

If you are working on any kind of code where you need the compiler to go through and re-read the same part more than one time, usually at least a few times, then the loops are going to be helpful. We will take a look at how you are able to do this, without having to re-write the same line or lines of code a bunch of times.

Sure, you can definitely go through and code all that you want without these loops. You can just rewrite all of the lines repeatedly. This may not seem like a big deal if you just need it to repeat two or three times. However, what if the code could potentially repeat itself a hundred times or more? You can do this with the loop and it really isolates takes a lesser line of code, rather than potentially hundreds if you do not use the loop.

There are many examples of working with these loops in your code. Let us say that you are working on some kind of code where you want it to list out all of the numbers from one to ten but you do not want to waste your time writing out all of the lines of code to make this happen. The loop is going to be able to help you get it all done without having to write so much or making the code into a big mess in the process.

The process of working with these loops is going to be so much easier than it sounds in the beginning, and it will not take long before you start to really appreciate them in your own code. They are there to talk with the compiler and tell it that instead of moving on to the next part; it needs to repeat that certain part of code until some conditions are met. You will be the one to determine what conditions the compiler needs to meet before it moves on from the loop. To help us get a better understanding of how these loops work, we will take a look at a few examples of loops that you are able to work with.

This brings us to the next point. When you are writing out the loops, you need to make sure that there is always a condition set up. If you forget to put in this condition or assume that you do not really need one, then your program is not going to work right. If everything else is set up properly, but the condition is missing, the compiler will continue to re-read the same part of code repeatedly, with no idea about when it should start. Your program will effectively be frozen at that point.

Think about how much space and time this is going to save you. When you work with some of the previous examples of coding that we have talked about, you would be responsible for writing out each line of code that you need. If you need to have the program count from one to ten, then you would have to repeat the code in this manner. However, since you are basically doing the same thing, and you just want the compiler to repeat the same thing, you will be able to work with the loop in order to make this happen.

This is one of the best things when it comes to learning how to use a loop. You no longer have to write it all out and can easily combine a lot of lines of code into just a few, and make sure that the right words are placed into the code so that the compiler knows how many times you want it to go through that part of the code. With one or two lines of code, the loops can get a ton of coding done in the process for you.

As you work through your Python language, you will find that there are actually quite a few loops that are available for you to try out, based on what kind of program you would like to write. The three main types that we are going to take a look at including the nested loop, the while loop, and the for a loop. Let us take a look at how these each work, how they are similar, and some of the differences that come with them.

What is the while loop

Out of the three-loop types that we talked about above, we are going to start our study off with the while loop. This type of loop is one that you will choose any time that you know how many iterations of the cycle that you want the code to go through and you want to make sure the compiler reads through at least that many times. If you want to make sure that the compiler reads through the loop at least one time, for example, then you will want to work with the while loop to make this happen.

With the while loop, your goal is not to make the code go through its cycle an indefinite amount of times, but you do want to make sure that it goes through for a specific number of times. If you are counting from one to ten, you want to make sure it goes through the loop ten times to be right. With this option, the loop is going to go through at least one time and then check to see if the conditions are met or not. Therefore, it will put up the number one, then check its conditions and put up number two, and so on until it sees where it is.

To give us a little bit better of an understanding on how these loops work, let us take a glimpse at a few sample codes of the while loop and see what happens:

counter = 1
while(counter <= 3):

    principal = int(input("Enter the principal amount:"))

    numberofyeras = int(input("Enter the number of years:"))

rateofinterest = float(input("Enter the rate of interest:"))

*simpleinterest = principal * numberofyears * rateofinterest/100*

print("Simple interest = %.2f" %simpleinterest)

#increase the counter by 1

counter = counter + 1

print("You have calculated simple interest for 3 time!")

Now that we have a better idea of what the while loop is going to look like, make sure to stop here and add the code above into your compiler and then let it execute. When this one is done, the output is going to be set up in a way that the user is able to place in any information that they want into this program. Once that is done, the program is going to go through the computations necessary, and then can see the interest rates, the final amounts, and more based on the numbers that your user, or yourself, decided to add into the system.

With the example that we used above, we made it so that the while loop would go through three times. This means that the user is allowed to put in the input of their choice three times, and then this part of the program will be done. As the programmer, you are able to go through and make some changes, adding in more loops, for example, to ensure that this program works the way that you want it to work.

Moving on to the for loop

Another option that you are able to work with when it comes to the idea of loops in Python is known as the for a loop. The for loop is going to work in a lot of different situations, especially when you just want the program to repeat as many times as it needs to in order to get the work done. This for loop is more common to see because it can often cover a lot of the same things that the while loop can, and it is seen as the more traditional form of this process.

With the for loop, you will have it set up so that the user isn't the one who goes in and gives the program information that determines when the loop will stop. Instead, the for loop is set up to go over the iteration in the order that things show up inside your statement, and then this information is going to show up on your screen. There is not any need for input from an outside force or user, at least until it reaches the end. An example of the code that you can use to work on a for loop includes:

```
# Measure some strings:
words = ['apple', 'mango', 'banana', 'orange']
for w in words:
print(w, len(w))
```

If you decide to work with the example that we have of a for loop above, you can take a moment to type it into your compiler and see what shows up on the screen when this executes. When you do this, the four fruits are going to show up on the screen, appearing in the same order that they are written out above. You do have the choice to change them up in terms of the order or how many are there, but once they are placed into the code, they are going to stay there, and changes are not allowed.

What the nested loop is all about

Now that we have had a chance to look at the while loop and the loop, it is time to work on the third and final loop known as the nested loop. This one is a bit different compared to the other two, but you will find that there can be a lot of situations where this loop is going to be the most helpful. When you do work with the nested loop, you are going to put one loop in with another loop, and then you will allow both of these loops to run together until they are done with their job.

This may seem like a strange thing to add to your code, but there are actually a lot of times when this is going to work out well with the code that you are trying to write. For example, you may decide that a game or another program you are writing needs something like a multiplication table. You can use the idea of the nested loop in order to make sure the code writes out the whole table going from one to ten and includes all of the answers that you need to have to go with each part.

This would be a huge amount of code if you wrote out each line to tell the program how to behave. And you can certainly do that if you want to waste some time practicing your code writing. However, a better method to use to make this work, a way that would get it done in relatively few lines of code and save you, time includes the following:

#write a multiplication table from 1 to 10

For x in xrange(1, 11):

For y in xrange(1, 11):

Print '%d = %d' % (x, y, x*x)

When you got the output of this program, it is going to look similar to this:

1*1 = 1

1*2 = 2

1*3 = 3

1*4 = 4

All the way, up to 1*10 = 2

Then it would move on to do the table by twos such as this:

2*1 =2

2*2 = 4

And so on until you end up with 10*10 = 100 as your final spot in the sequence.

Go ahead, put this into the compiler, and see what happens. You will simply have four lines of code, and end up with a whole multiplication table that shows up on your program. Think of how many lines of code you would have to scribble out to get this table the traditional way that you did before? This table only took a few lines to accomplish, which shows how powerful and great the nested loop can be.

As you can see, there are many times when you may decide to use these loops and see how well they are able to fit into your code. There are many times when you will need to make a loop and add it to the code in order to get more things done, without a mess and without having to use a lot of code writing in the process. Try out some of the codes in this chapter and see how to work with the loops and how you can add this into your code.

Chapter 9: Classes and Objects in Python

One of the things that you are going to enjoy when it comes to using the Python language is that it is made up of classes and objects. We are going to get into more details about what all of this means and why this is important, but remember that this is going to really help you to keep things organized, and can keep your code easier to write out.

Classes and objects are important to learn how to work with because inside of the code, they are going to be there to ensure you can sort through all of the different parts found in the code. They are also going to make sure that when you save any of the parts of your code, you will be able to find them in the right spot again, without any movement when it is time to get the code to execute the code when it is time.

The objects are important as well because they will be what defines the different parts of the code, which helps you and the person using the code understand what is being done there. You still need to work with the classes as well because the class is in charge of holding onto the classes. With that introduction in mind, it is time for us to learn how to create our own objects and classes, and how to make these work together.

Creating a class in Python

The first thing that we need to take a look at is how to create one of the classes in the Python language. This is not something that the Python language is going to be able to do for you so you need to make sure you learn how to do it. Once you can create your own classes, you will be able to use them to organize the code and will ensure that none of the objects will end up lost in the process. The best way to get the classes made though is to make sure that you use the right keywords, and then come up with the name of the class.

The neat thing about working with this one is that you will gain a bit of freedom when you use this one. You can give the class that you create any kind of name that you would like. However, the thing for you to keep in mind with doing this is that the name needs to come after the keyword. It can also help you to come up with a name for the class that you are able to remember later when you need to pull that class up.

After you have been able to name a particular class that you are working on, then it is time to work with the subclass that comes with it. This subclass is going to be easy to find because it is going to be found inside the parenthesis of the code after the name of the class. Your job here is to make sure that when you are naming the subclass you add it to the parenthesis, and then add in a semicolon as well. While your code will work just fine without the semicolon, using it is considered part of the proper coding protocol.

If you are just starting out with the idea of the classes and objects, you may worry that creating one of these classes is going to be hard. You are responsible for creating pretty much a container that will help hold onto many different objects. How are you going to write in some code that helps to get all of this done and working together

This may seem complicated, but like with some of the other codes that are in this guidebook, once we look at some of the examples of how to do this, you will be able to see some great results and will find it is not as complicated as it seems. Let us examine at an example of the syntax that you are able to use when it is time to create one of your own classes:

class Vehicle(object):

#constructor

def_init_(self, steering, wheels, clutch, breaks, gears):

self._steering = steering

self._wheels = wheels

self._clutch = clutch

self._breaks =breaks

self._gears = gears

#destructor

def_del_(self):

   print("This is destructor....")

```
#member functions or methods

def Display_Vehicle(self):

    print('Steering:' , self._steering)

    print('Wheels:', self._wheels)

    print('Clutch:', self._clutch)

    print('Breaks:', self._breaks)

    print('Gears:', self._gears)

#instantiate a vehicle option

myGenericVehicle = Vehicle('Power Steering', 4, 'Super Clutch', 'Disk Breaks', 5)


myGenericVehicle.Display_Vehicle()
```

Before we move on with this one, we need to take the time to add this into a

compiler and see what happens. Just open up the text editor that you are working

with and type up the code that we have above. As you write this out, see if you are

able to recognize a few of the different topics that we have discussed already in

this guidebook! Once you have finished typing this code in, it is time to look at

the different parts.

We need to divide this up a bit and take a closer look at how it is all going to work

together. Our first goal here is to look at the class definition and how it is going to

show up in the code. This definition of the class is important because it is where

you can instantiate the object, and then you can add the definition back into the class. The reason for all of this is that you will be able to write it out so that the class is written and is able to hold onto any objects that you place inside.

When you work with the class definition, it is important to pay attention to what you define it as because this part will tell the compiler what it needs to do. If you are looking to get a new definition of the class added into the code, you have a few functions to make this happen. The two that work the best for this include object_attribute and object_method, to make sure that the definition works the best for you.

After we have worked with the class definition, it is time to look at with these classes will include the special attributes. These special attributes are going to be important with this one because they will provide you with a bit of extra security that the code is going to work the way that you want, without errors and other issues along the way.

In the code that we were doing before has some of the special attributes. We used this in order to make sure that the classes and the objects were going to end up in the right spot each time. That is just one example of a special attribute that works with classes. A few of the other options that you can learn about when you want to create your own classes include:

- ___bases___: this is considered a tuple that contains any of the superclasses

- __module__: this is where you are going to find the name of the module and it will also hold your classes.

- __name__: this will hold on to the class name.

- __doc__: this is where you are going to find the reference string inside the document for your class.

- __dict__: this is going to be the variable for the dict. Inside the class name.

Now that we have had a chance to look at the special attributes that go with creating a class, it is time to look at another thing that will help us. This part is going to help us to access a few of the members that come in the class that you just created. This needs to be done in order to ensure that the compiler and the text editor are able to recognize the new class that you created and that it will show up in your program as well. To help you see the way that you are able to access the members of any class that has been created, you can use a code like the way below:

```
class Cat(object)
    itsAge = None
    itsWeight = None
    itsName = None
    #set accessor function use to assign values to the fields or member vars
    def setItsAge(self, itsAge):
    self.itsAge = itsAge
```

```python
def setItsWeight(self, itsWeight):

    self.itsWeight = itsWeight


def setItsName(self, itsName):

    self.itsName =itsName


#get accessor function use to return the values from a field

def getItsAge(self):

    return self.itsAge

def getItsWeight(self):

    return self.itsWeight


def getItsName(self):

    return self.itsName


objFrisky = Cat()

objFrisky.setItsAge(5)

objFrisky.setItsWeight(10)

objFrisky.setItsName("Frisky")

print("Cats Name is:", objFrisky.getItsname())

print("Its age is:", objFrisky.getItsAge())

print("Its weight is:", objFrisky.getItsName())
```

Take a moment to type this into your compiler and have it run. You are going to be able to see the results of the code show up on your screen right away. This is going to include things like the name of the cat, as Frisky, along with all of the other things that we had placed in there. You do have the freedom to add in different options and experiment a bit to see what is going to happen as you do that.

You can see that a class is not going to be that difficult to work with. They are the perfect thing to use in order to take care of all the different information that is in your code and to keep it all in order so that it comes up when you want, and in the right order. You are able to create any kind of class as you would, and fill it up with any of the objects that you would like. If you use the syntax above as your guide for making classes, you will be set to get these done in no time.

A look at the objects.

Now that we have had some time to look at the classes that you are able to write out in your code, it is time to look at some of the objects, and how these two topics are going to relate back to one another. To keep this simple, the objects are going to be the part of the code that you will place into the classes that you are going to create.

You can have as many objects as you would like in your code, and you can fit as many of them into each class as you would like. But there are a few rules that you should go with to make sure it all falls in line with what is allowed with the code.

First, when you are creating a class, it can be any kind that you would like. And you can add in any kind of object that you would like. Keep in mind that in one class, you need to make sure, when someone looks at it; it makes sense why all of those objects are in the same class. They do not have to be exactly the same; you could have a class that is all animals, rather than just ones that are elephants. But it needs to make sense why all of the items are in the same class.

Working with objects and classes are going to help you to really see some results with the kind of code that you want to right. The classes are going to hold onto all of the different objects that you are going into the code, and will ensure that you are able to get things to show up at the right time when your code is ready to execute. Experiment a bit with the code by adding it into your compiler to make sure that you are able to create the classes and the objects that you would like to make in your codes.

Chapter 10: The Python Iterators

The Python iterators are a fun thing to add into your code if it is going to work with the kind of program that you will need. The iterators in Python are going to be any kind of object that you add into the code that is going to allow for an iteration over a collection. Now, you will find that these collections do not have to object that is found in the computer memory, and because of this, it is possible to make some objects that are infinite if you choose.

Let us be a bit more precise with the definition that we are using. You can easily say that an iterable is an item that has an "__inter__' method needed in returning an iterator object. IT is also possible that an iterator is an object containing the '__inter__' method and the '__next__' or you can use simply 'next'. When you look at the former, you are going to get an iterator object and then the latter is going to return the subsequent elements of the iteration.

When you work on your code, you want to avoid calling 'next' and __inter__ directly. Python is going to help you call these up automatically if you use a list or 'for' comprehensions. In case you do need to go through and call them up manually, you can use the included in the functions of 'inter' and 'next' in Python and then pass the container or iterator as the restriction.

Yes, this one does seem to be a bit more complicated, but if you are using the Python language to work with some mathematics, you will love working with these iterators. Python is a great language that has libraries and more that can support the mathematics that you would like to use. For example, you can use things like notations, tuples, sets, and lists to help you get mathematical things done in this language.

The biggest thing that you may like when you decide to work with Python if you have a mind that is mathematical is these iterators, as well as the generators that we talked about at an earlier time in this guidebook. Both the iterator and the generator can help to make it easier for the programmer to go through and write out some more complex code. To help us see some of the different things that you are able to do when you introduce the iterator in the Python code that you are writing.

Understanding what iterators are all about

We spent a bit of time above talking about what iterators are, but we are going to dive into this a bit more and see what they are and how you are able to use them in your code. To keep things simple, the iterator is going to be any kind of object that you add into your code that is able to iterate throughout the collection. The collection can be new objects that you create or ones that are found in the memory already.

The tables that you use in the code are going to be defined as objects that are going to call on the method known as __iter__, and this is going to be the method that you want to return back to the object that is your iterator. In this case, it is possible to get this kind of iterator to work with two methods at the same time. The two methods that work with this one include the __iter__ and the __next__ method. With the __next__ method, you will need to use it any time that you want to get the method to return to the object of the iterator. However, with the other one, you are going to ask the compiler to return the element that ends up in the iterator. Because the iterator is going to be its own iterator, it is always going to be able to return the method of __self-_ in the method of the iterator.

Now, at this point, we need to make sure that our code is working well, and to make sure that the things inside the code still make sense when you are coding. To make this happen, programmers will usually choose to not bring out either of the methods directly in their code. Instead, they are going to work with the list comprehension. Python will go through and automatically set this up. However, double-check on this because depending on the code, you may need to do a bit of manual work to get it called up, using a few special functions found in Python.

At this point in the process, we need to actually look at the steps that you are able to take in order to work with the iterators in Python. We are going to make the letter "b" be iterable that we want. If this is our iterable, you would be able to write out either iter(b) or d.__iter__() to get the answer or to make the code work. Either of these is fine and the compiler will read them the same, but the first option is going to be simpler to read and write out.

A note to keep in mind here is that when you decide to work with what is known as the len) function, the iterator is not going to have a defined length that you are able to use here. This is going to be true most of the time when you try to do some iterators in Python. However, the good news is that with the len() function, it isn't very often that you will use it at all. If you do need to bring it out, you can look inside the iterator and see the number of items inside of it, then do the work manually to get it to work.

An example of how these iterators work:

Some tables will contain other objects, which will serve as their iterators, and this means that they are not going to be iterators themselves. For instance, the object 'list" is iterable but not at all an iterator (instead of implementing next, it is going to implement __inter__). As you can see in the example that we are going to have below, iterators for the 'list' objects are going to use 'listiterator' type. You may even observe how the 'list' objects contained a properly establish length, and the listiterato objects do not have that.

>>> a = [1, 2]
>>> type(a)

>>>type(iter(a))

<type'listiterator'>

>>>it = itera)

>>>next(it)

1

>>>next(it)

2

>>>next(it)

Traceback (most recent call last):

File "<stdin>", line 1, in <module>

StopIteration

>>>len(a)

2

>>>len(it)

Traceback(most recent call last):

File "<stdin>", line 1, in <module>

TypeError: object of type 'listiterator' has no len()

When this iterator is all done and typed into the compiler well, the interpreter is going to expect it to come out with an exception raised. This particular exception is going to be called "StopIteration". However, when you are working with an iterator, it is technically going to keep going over a set that is endless. These are going to be able to dictate that the user should make sure they are not using the program in any manner that creates a loop that keeps going on and on. You may find that manually fixing this can be the best bet to ensure that any loops you add

into the code won't get stuck and freeze up your program.

Chapter 11: Starting with the Python Generators

The next idea that we are going to take a look at here is the idea of the generators. The generators that show up in Python are going to be functions that will ensure you can create a sequence of results. The reason that we look at them is that the generators are able to maintain a state that is known as their local state, ensuring that the function is able to resume right back where they left off if they had to be called up more than one time.

This may sound a bit confusing, but as you work through a few of the different codes that we study in this guidebook, you will find that it starts to make a bit more sense as time goes on. You can think of the generator as a really strong and powerful iterator. The function state will be maintained as we talked about before when you bring in the keyword of "yield". In Python, this is similar to hitting the return button, but we do need to explore a few of the differences, as well as more information on how these generators can come into play in your codes.

How to make these generators work?

There are many things that the generator is going to be able to do when it comes to making your code behave, and ensuring that you do not have to restart the code all over again when you call up a function more than once. However, you will find that one of the best ways to make sure that we have a full understanding of how these generators work is to look at an example, such as the one we will provide to you below:

```
# generator_example_1.py

Def numberGenerator(n):
    Number = 0
    While number < n:
    Yield number
    Number + = 1

myGenerator = numberGenerator(3)

print(next(myGenerator))
print(next(myGeneartor))
print(next(myGenerator))
```

The code that we have above is going to define a generator for you with the name 'numberGenerator' that gest the value 'n' as the argument before you go through and define it using a while loop to help with a limit value. In addition, it is going through and helping you define a variable that has the name of 'number' and then it assigns a zero value with this.

When you call in your instantiated generator using the 'myGenerator with the method 'next()' in it, it is going to go through and run your generator through the code until the initial 'yield' statement. For this example, it is going to return 1. Even when you get a value returned to you, your function is going to tend to keep the variable 'number' value for when you call up your function next, and then it grows in value by one. What this means is that it is able to start up again right where it left off at the next call of the function.

Now, it is possible for you to call up a generator once more after this. If this is what you decide to do, you just need to keep following what we have already placed into the code, but then this is going raise up an exception. This exception is going to say "StopIteration" simply because it has finished up and reverted from the internal while loop at this point.

This may make it seem frustrating and like you are not able to do what you want with the code, but this can be useful when it comes to adding this into your code. The use of the generator in this manner is going to help you create a few of the iterables that you need as you go through this.

Let us say that you have gone through on your code and you were able to use the list() to wrap 'myGenerator'. When this happens, you are going to get an array of numbers back as the answer, rather than the generator object that you would like. In some instances though, this is going to make life a bit easier for you to do and work with.

Looking at how between and yield are going to be different.

It is time to look at another point that shows up when you work with the generators. There will be times in this process where the "return" keyword is going to be the one to use. This is going to happen when you want to get a return of a value from the given function. When you do this, the function is going to get lost out of the local state and this can make it difficult to run the code that you want.

What all of this is going to mean is that when you go through and need to call up the function once more, or as frequently as you would like, the code will not have a reference point to call up. You will have to go and start all the way from the top in the first statement. You can easily see why this is going to cause some problems if you are not careful.

Then there is the option of using the keyword of 'yield'. This one is going to be brought out when you want to make sure that you want to keep the state of the function, without having to start all the way over. You can choose when you want to go back with the function or when it is time to start over, giving you a bit more control, this is why using the generators, and working with the yield keyword can be really useful for many of your codes.

The returned generator

The generator can use the statement for 'return' but only when there is no return value. The generator will then go on as in any other function return when it reaches this statement. The return tells the program that you are done and you want it to go back to the rest of the code. Let us take a look at how you can change up the code to use these generators simply by adding in an if-else clause so that you can discriminate against any numbers that are above 20. The code you would use for this includes:

```python
# geneator_example_2.py

def numberGeneator(n):
    if n < 20:
    number = 0
    while number < n:
    yield number
    number +=1
else:
    return
print(list(numberGeneator(30)))
```

This particular example is going to show that the genitor will be an empty array. This is because we have set it so that it will not yield any values that are above 20. Since 30 is above 20, you will not get any results with this one. In this particular case, the return statement is going to work in the same way as a break statement. However, if you go through this code and you get a value that is below 20, you would then see that show up in the code.

More to learn about the generators

The thing to remember with these generators is that they are a type of iterator, an iterator that the code has been able to define with a notation of the function so that the function is easier to use in the code. When you decide to work with the generator, you are basically working with a type of function that is able to give you a yield expression. These will not be able to give you the return value that you may expect though.

Instead of doing this, when it is time to use the generators, they are going to just provide you with the results. The process that you should remember with this is that you need the generator to be an automated process in Python otherwise; it is going to become too complicated and may not work.

Now, you will find that there are a few options that you can use when it comes to calling up any generator that is available for you to use. If you call up the generator using the __next__ keyword, the yield you are going to get will show up in the next iteration value in the line. This is not the only option that is available though and you can work with the __iter__, which is one that will make sure your program is implemented automatically while telling the program that it needs to take the generator and move it back to the place where the iterator is needed.

As you go through and work on your code and you find that you need to add in a generator at some point, there are going to be a few options to choose from to make it easier. Some of the different options that you are able to work with include:

1. Generator expressions: These expressions are helpful to work with because they will help the programmer to define the generator with the help of simple notation. This is easier, and you can easily do it any time that you create a list using the Python language. You can use the two methods that we have above, the __next__ and __iter__ to make it happen because these provide you with the results for any type of generator that you want to create.

2. Recursive generators: It is possible for your chosen generator to be recursive, just like what you are able to find with some functions. The idea that you get with this one is that you would need to swap out all of the elements that you have on your list with the one that ends up on top. This helps all of the elements to move up and the list will slowly start to disappear as you do this.

When are some times that I need generators?

We have spent some time in this chapter talking about generators and how you are able to use them, but now it is time to take a look at when you might actually use the generators to help you get things done. We did a few examples of these generators through this guidebook, and you can see that they are a more advanced tool that can be used to write out codes.

As a beginner, it is possible that you will not use these generators all that much. It may seem like they are too difficult, but knowing how to make them work can ensure that there is some kind of efficiency when it comes to the program you are trying to write. Some of the scenarios where you may find that using these generators is going to be helpful can include the following:

1. Any time that you as the programmer end up with a ton of data that you think needs to be processed. The generators help with this because they are going to be able to offer a calculation based on the demand. This is a good option to use when you want to finish a project like stream processing.

2. You may find that working with a stacked generator can mean that you are working with the process of piping. This is the same way that you would be able to use the Unix pipes. To make this easier, you are able to use the generator in order to pipeline a series of operations to make it easier to work with.

As you can see, the generators are going to be a wonderful addition to the process that allows you to have a lot of freedom in what you are doing, can make sure that you are able to get back to the part of the code where you want to be, and can generally make your life easier rather than having to plan for the code restarting all of the time. It may be a bit more than what some beginners want to add into their codes, but it can make a world of difference in how efficient and easy your code is to work with.

Chapter 12: Is It Important to Work with Assert Handling with Python?

Now it is time to take our work in a different direction. We are going to take some time to learn about assertions in Python. These are somewhat similar to what we have looked at with a few other topics, but it is still important to discover the differences that come with it. You will see that assertions are most likely to come up when exception handling is discussed, and often you will need to handle both of these topics at the same time. This is why we are going to take some time to look at assert handling now.

When we talk about assertion within the Python language, we are looking at something that is kind of like a check for how well the code is going to work. Either you can choose to have it off or one when you are completed with the testing portion of your program. The effortless way to think about an affirmation is that it is like a raise if statement or a raise if not statement. If you are testing the exception, and you end up with the latter one showing up, you will notice that the exception has been raised in the program.

You will need to use the assert statement in order to help make sure the assertion is carried out. This is going to be a newer keyword, and you may not be able to find it in some of the older versions of Python if you choose to go with these. Many programs find that it is easiest to place the assertions at the way beginning of the function because this helps you to double-check the function and see if it has an input that is valid. They may also put it after calling up a function to check if the output is valid to use as well.

Looking more at the assert statement

When you are working to add in one of these assert statements in any code, the program in Python is set up to evaluate the expression that follows this statement. The hope here is that the answer is true and you will get to move on with the code. However, there are going to be times when the statement is going to evaluate the part of the code and will find that the expression is false. This is when the exception is known as AssertionError. The syntax that we will see when using this one includes:

assert Expression [, Arguments]

If you use this and the assertion fails, Python is going to use ArgumentExression as your argument for this error. These types of exceptions can be caught, and you can handle them similarly, to what we did earlier with exception handling. You can employ the try-except statement to help you deal with it properly.

There will be times when the Python code will not be able to handle the exception that is raised with that statement. If the program cannot handle it, then it is going to terminate your program and will produce a traceback. However, for the most part, this assertion is going to help you handle any issues that come up and it is mostly there to help you catch anything that can go wrong in the program.

Learning how to do assertion handling is going to be important to any type of code that you choose to write. It is going to make sure that if there is an issue inside of your code, you are able to catch it and handle it before you send that program out to the world. It gives you the option of checking out if the statement you wrote is true or not whether the program is able to handle this on its own, or if it is time to fix a few errors or bugs that, you may have made inside of that program.

No matter why you decide to use it, or whether or not it finds the bug or mistake that is there (sometimes there are no bugs or mistakes), assertions can be helpful. This is even truer if you are working with any kind of exception in the code. It is effective, it is safe, and it only adds a few more lines of code overall to make sure that the whole program is going to work in the proper manner.

Why should I take the time to test my code?

One of the things that you are able to do with the assert statement is to test your code in certain areas and make sure that it works. It gets the program to go through and perform a test so that you catch bugs or potential problems before you release the program. Getting used to not only writing the code but also writing out some testing code and running it with the regular code can make sure that your program always works the way that you want.

When you are able to use this process in the proper manner, you will find that the assert statements are going to be a good way to help you define the intent of any code you write and to make sure that it works the way that you want. However, if you are still uncertain about why you need to work with assert statements, there are many great rules to follow, including:

1. When you pick out the unit that you are going to use in the testing, you want to make sure this unit is able to keep its focus on the functionality that the code has. Its job is to prove that this part of the code works properly and is correct.

2. You will do many different units and each of them needs to work on their own, rather than together. Each of the tests that you write need to be able to run on their own, along with the test suite, even if they are called up in a different order.

   a. The idea with this kind of rule is that your test should be loaded up with a new data set and it needs to clean up as well when it is done. The two methods that you can add to your assert statement to make this happen to include the setup() method and the teardown() method.

3. When you are designing a new test, you need to make sure that the code you write is able to run fairly quickly. If it does not, then this is really going

to slow down what you are able to do with the code. Complex data and more can slow this process down, but you want to make sure that the test is able to go through and do the work that you want, without slowing the program down that you are working on.

4. There are many different tools that you are able to work within your programming, and it is important to learn how to use them as well as possible. You also want to make sure that the tests are set up as often as possible. Do so automatically and at any time that you stop to save the code to make sure that your code works well.

5. Before you start with a new session of the coding, you need to go through and do a full test suite run. And when you are all done, go through and run that test again. This helps you to add in some more confidence about the code you are writing and ensures that nothing is broken before or after a code writing session.

6. If you are working on a development session and then have to leave right in the middle, you can write in a broken unit test about what you are planning on working on next. Then, when you come back to the work, you will still have a point there where you can get right back on track.

7. When you are doing code and trying to debug it, you should work on a new test that is responsible for finding the bug. This is not always something that is possible, but the bug-catching tests are going to be very valuable when you do your project.

8. When you are testing out a function, make sure that you use descriptive and long names. The style guide for this point is often going to be a bit

different than what you would do when running a code; for those, you want names that are somewhat short. The reason that your testing functions need to be longer is that you want them to display on the screen when the test fails. When you have them as descriptive as possible, it is easier to tell what is going on in the code.

9. Anytime that you are doing something with your code, and it does not function the way that you want it to, or you need to make sure that something gets changed, and you have already been able to do the testing, this means that the testing suite can be used here to fix this problem. The testing code needs to be read as much if not more than the code you decide to run.

    a. Now, it is not necessarily a bad thing to rely on the testing code to help you out. However, taking the right precautions and making sure that you test the code to check for the accuracy of the code.

10. Another way that you are able to use the testing code to make sure that everything lines up well is to introduce another developer to the mix. They are going to look through the testing code and double-check things for you. Since they are not close to the code at all and have not been working with it, they will be a fresh pair of eyes to ensure that you will be able to catch all of the bugs and other issues that come with it.

It is tempting to avoid some of the testings that need to be done with your code. But doing this kind of testing is going to make sure that any code you decide to work with is free of errors or any bugs so that it works well. You should make sure that you use the assert statement rules that we have above, and you will be able to

always test your code and make sure that it works the way that you would like

from the beginning.

Chapter 13: Using Closures Properly in Python to Get Your Codes Done

The next item that we need to take a look at when we try to develop a code in Python is the idea of closures. However, before we jump into this too far, we need to be able to understand a few of the other parts that come with the Python language. Nested functions and non-local variables are going to be needed with this kind of code, and they will help us to really work on the closures and get them to work well for us. With this in mind, we are going to first take a look at the nested functions.

First, what is a nested function? Any time that you have one function that you want to use and you need to define it inside of a different kind of function, the first one is going to be established as the nested function. These nested functions are going to be interesting to work with because of how you create them and their ability to approach variables of the enclosing scope. In Python, though the non-local variables can be accessed only when you are in the current scope, and any scope that is not there will not be able to find them. Let us examine at an example of how this is going to work:

 # Python program to illustrate

 # nested functions

def outerFunction(text):

```
    text = text

    def innerFunction():

        print(text)


    innerFunction()


if __name__ == '__main__':

    outerFunction('Hey!')
```

As you can see here, the innerFunction() part of the code is something that your outerFunction can access, and you can use it as much as you want as long as you are in that function. However, if you leave this, or go to another part of the code, you will not be able to access that innerFunction() part. In this case, the innerFunction() is going to be the nested function, which will use text as its non-local variable.

What are these closures?

Now that we have had a chance to look at the nested function and see what they are, as well as a look at the non-local variables, it is time to bring in the idea of the closure. The closure is going to be an object of the function that is responsible for remembering the values that you add into the enclosing scope. This is going to happen, even when the objects will not show up in the memory of the computer that you use.

The closure is going to be like a new record that is responsible for storing the function, along with the environment and we can look at it as a mapping that associates all of the variables in the function that ends up being free. As we go through with this, remember that the variables that are found here are going to be used locally, but they will be defined in their enclosing scope. You are able to do this thanks to the value or the reference that you bound to the namespace of the closure the first time that you created it.

If you have worked with the plain function in the past, you will find that the closure is going to be a bit different. The closure comes in and makes it so that the function is able to access the variables that you end up capturing, and it does this by going through the closures copies of the references or its copies of the values. This is possible and can happen even when the function is called up outside of its own scope. Let us take a glimpse at how this is going to work and some of the things that you can do to get the best results.

 # Python program to illustrate

 # closures

def outerFunction(text):

   text = text

```python
def innerFunction():

    print(text)


    return innerFunction # Note we are returning function WITHOUT
parenthesis

if __name__ == '__main__':
    myFunction = outerFunction('Hey!')
    myFunction()
```

Take a moment to type this code into your compiler and see what happens. What you should be able to observe from this code is that the closure is there to help you call the function up, even when you are not in the right scope. The function is known as innerFunction(has its scope present only in your outerFunction. However, when you use one of these closures, as we did before, you are able to extend the scope so you can call it up anywhere that you would like.

The code above did the same thing that we did originally; make it so that the nested function is called up only inside its original function. However, if you want to be able to call up the function at any point, even when you are outside its scope, you would need to use a code like this one:

```python
# Python program to illustrate
# closures
```

```python
import logging
logging.basicConfig(filename='example.log', level=logging.INFO)


def logger(func):
    def log_func(*args):
        logging.info(
            'Running "{}" with arguments {}'.format(func.__name__, args))
        print(func(*args))
    # Necessary for closure to work (returning WITHOUT parenthesis)
    return log_func


def add(x, y):
    return x+y


def sub(x, y):
    return x-y


add_logger = logger(add)
sub_logger = logger(sub)


add_logger(3, 3)
add_logger(4, 5)
```

sub_logger(10, 5)

sub_logger(20, 10)

If you are curious about the differences that show up in the two codes that we have just done, you can take a look at how they react when brought up in your compiler. When you do this, you are going to see that the output between the two will be a bit different, which is going to help you see how these closures work so well in your code. Learning how these works in a similar manner and how they are different will make it much easier for you to use them no matter what scope you have in mind.

The biggest decision that you need to make when you are using this is whether you would like the chance to reach the nested function only when it is inside of the original function you placed it, would you like the option, or will need the option, to reach it no matter where you are in the code. For the first option, you just need to work with the first code earlier in this chapter, and for the second one, you need to make sure that the closure is there to help you, like what we just did above.

When is a closure necessary?

As we have been able to talk about a bit in this guidebook, there are a few different situations where you would need to add some kind of closure into the code that you are writing. However, we will go over them very quick to make sure you are familiar when they are going to come into play, and when they may be necessary for your success.

The first reason that you would want to use closures is that they can be a great callback function when needed. This means that you are able to use the closure to provide you with a manner of hiding any data that you want. In your code, this can reduce the number of global variables that are available, but this is a good thing. Reducing the number of those variables is going to reduce the bugs that show up and can make it cleaner and nicer.

Another benefit of working with these closures in your code is that they make the functions work better. If you have two or more functions that need to work at the same time or really close together, the closures are an efficient and good manner to deal with all of them. However, if the number of functions gets too high, and you need to work with quite a few of them in your code, you will need to result in the classes instead.

The best way to tell if you need to work with a closure or not is the end result that you want to see when it is all done. Some programmers find that there really isn't a need for them to access the nested function other than in the current scope, so they would not need to work with the closures and adding one in is more time and work than necessary.

Then there are going to be times when the closures are necessary to make the code work the way that you would like. If you need the function to not only show up in your local scope if this is something that your code needs to see happen, then working with the closure is going to make this happen in a more successful manner.

Chapter 14: Creating Your Own Inheritances

Inheritances are another neat idea that you are able to create when working on your own Python code. This one is going to take some writing out and may seem a bit longer and more work compared to the others, but once it gets put into the code, you will find that it actually helps the code to flow easier, and will ensure that your code works the way that you would like.

When you bring out an inheritance that you want to work with, you will find that they are going to make sure that you can write out a ton of code that is complex, without having to go through and write out every line. This cleans up the code, helps it to look nicer, and can save you some time and effort all at the same time.

To help us get started when it comes to how these inheritances are going to work, we need to know what this is all about. The inheritance is going to be when you write out some code, and then you turn that into the parent code. You can then copy it down and make some changes, without changing up the original code, and make a brand new child code. The child code is completely adjustable along the way so that you are able to add and take things away as you need, and the parent code from before will still work the same.

You can go on down the line with this as well. You can just have one parent code and one child code, or you can make your own family tree of inheritances with this idea. Moreover, each child code is able to be adjusted and changed so that you end up with exactly what you need, without having any effect on the code that is being used as the parent.

While an inheritance may sound complex, it is a simple code to learn. You can add or take away as much as you want to get this code to work the way that you want. A good example of how an inheritance looks like inside of your code includes the following:

```
#Example of inheritance
#base class
class Student(object):
        def__init__(self, name, rollno):
        self.name = name
        self.rollno = rollno
#Graduate class inherits or derived from Student class
class GraduateStudent(Student):
        def__init__(self, name, rollno, graduate):
        Student__init__(self, name, rollno)
        self.graduate = graduate

def DisplayGraduateStudent(self):
        print"Student Name:", self.name)
        print("Student Rollno:", self.rollno)
```

```
print("Study Group:", self.graduate)


#Post Graduate class inherits from Student class
class PostGraduate(Student):
        def__init__(self, name, rollno, postgrad):
        Student__init__(self, name, rollno)
        self.postgrad = postgrad


        def DisplayPostGraduateStudent(self):
        print("Student Name:", self.name)
        print("Student Rollno:", self.rollno)
        print("Study Group:", self.postgrad)


#instantiate from Graduate and PostGraduate classes
        objGradStudent = GraduateStudent("Mainu", 1, "MS-Mathematics")
        objPostGradStudent = PostGraduate("Shainu", 2, "MS-CS")
        objPostGradStudent.DisplayPostGraduateStudent()
```

When you type this into your interpreter, you are going to get the results:

('Student Name:', 'Mainu')

('Student Rollno:', 1)

('Student Group:', 'MSC-Mathematics')

('Student Name:', 'Shainu')

('Student Rollno:', 2)

('Student Group:', 'MSC-CS')

As you are working on this code, you will love that the inheritance will provide you with some freedom. If you already have a code written out that you like many features of, and you want to reuse them, you can do this with the help of inheritances, without having to go through and write the code a bunch of times. In addition, you can take the new child or derived code and rewrite it and add in the features that you want, and you will love the different processes that are available with this option in Python.

Another thing to remember with the inheritances is that you can really go through and add in as many derived classes as you would like. The only rules here are that you keep going down the line in order with one another, and you use a syntax similar to the one above. If you can do this, your derived classes can fill up lots of lines of code if that is what works the best for the program you are writing at the time.

The ability to write out a ton of derived classes, if you need to, and to have as many of these as you would like is going to make things easier. And each of the new derived classes that you are working on gets the benefits of taking on features that you want from the base code above, or you can drop some if that makes the program work a bit better.

Can I override one of my base classes?

The next thing that we need to take a look at and discuss when we are creating our own inheritance is how we are able to override one of the base classes that we want to use. There may be some times when you will start to create a derived class, and then you want to change up some things by overriding the base class. Any time that you want to go through and change up some of the features in the base class to create your new derived class, you are going to want to do an override to make this happen.

It is actually a lot easier to work with than it sounds in the beginning, but it basically allows you to take a base class and create an inheritance into a derived class. And then the derived class can override things in order to become brand new and work the way that you want in the code. This ensures that with any new class you make based on the base class, you will get to keep what you want, and then get rid of the things that are in the way or are not working how you want.

The process of overloading

In addition to being able to override some of the objects that are found in the base class when doing inheritances, you are able to work with overloading. When it is time to bring in overloading, this means that you are trying to take one of the identifiers in the code and use it to define at least two methods overall and get that to work in the code.

For the most part, when you do your own override, you will just have two methods, but there may be some situations where you need to work with more than two. These two methods need to be placed in the same class, but the parameters are going to be different so that they can be running in different processes. This overloading process is going to work the best when you have these two methods doing work that follows different parameters so that they can run at the same time, but will not interfere with each other.

As a beginner, there are not that many instances where you will need to use the process of overloading. However, as you start to write some more codes and add into the complexity, this may be something that sneaks in more based on the kind of code and program that you are trying to create.

Some more things to know when it comes to inheritances

We need to take a moment to discuss a few more things about these inheritances and how you are able to work with them in the Python code. The first thing to explore here is how you are able to work with multiple inheritances at once. When you decide to do one of these inheritances, you will find that as you go down the levels, each one is going to share a few similarities with the others, but it is still possible to get to a new level and make the changes that are needed.

The multiple inheritances may take a few more steps to get the thing done, but you will find that they are going to be done in the same manner that we did the single one, and you can just add to that example when you want to create one. You just need to keep moving down the line until you are done with all of the inheritances that you want to create.

When you are working on a program where you will need to code multiple inheritances, you will need to take one class, which is again going to be that base class, and you will give it at least two child classes to get started. This is important as you work with growing your code because it is going to help you get the inheritances to go down as far as you would like.

Multiple inheritances can be as simple or as complicated as you would like to make them. When you work on them, you will be able to create a brand new class, which we will call Class C, and you got the information to create this new class from the previous one, or Class B. Then you can go back and find that Class B was the one that you created from information out of Class A. Each of these layers is going to contain some features that you like from the class ahead of it, and you can go as far into it as you would like. Depending on the code that you decide to write, you could have ten or more of these classes, each level having features from the previous one to keep it going.

While you are working to create multiple inheritances, remember that you can go down the levels, as many times as you would like, but you are not allowed to do what is known as a circular inheritance? You can have as many parent classes that turn into derived classes, but you cannot make it go in a circle, and then connect things from the top with this method, or you are going to end up with an error in the code along the way.

As you can see, there are many different things that you are able to do with these inheritances. It can help you to save some time using the features that you like from the parent class, and it will ensure that you are able to clean up the code. Yes, the code example that we did above may look long, but it was there to give us an idea of how to work with the classes, both the base and the derived. In addition, if you had to write these out without using the idea of inheritances, imagine how many lines of code you have to write.

As you start to write more and more codes and make your own programs with the help of the Python language, you will find that there are going to be some inheritance types that you are able to use, because these are pretty popular. There are many times when you can just use the base code and use it to make a new piece of code, without having to waste a lot of time in order to rewrite the code again all of the time. It is as simple as this and can make your code really work well, without as much work.

Chapter 15: Bringing in the Descriptors

Another topic that we need to take a look at when working in the Python language is the idea of the descriptors. These descriptors come up a lot in your codes so it is a good idea for us to learn how to make these work. You can write some codes without these, but many times adding the descriptors to your code can help you to get a nice edge over the competition when you are working on any code that you would like. With this in mind though, they are sometimes a bit difficult to understand. This is why we are going to focus on a practical example to show us exactly how and when we would try to use these descriptors in one of our Python codes.

Imagine that you are trying to work with a new program that needs to be able to do some strict type checking of all the object attributes that show up. Since we see that Python is known as a dynamic language, there is not really support available for type checking, but this does not mean that you are stuck here. You are able to create your own program with the help of the descriptors that will help you to get this done.

Of course, it would be easier to work with some of the conventional methods and have the program do this for you. However, this is not available when you are working with Python, and any of the options that this language provides to you will not work in the right manner. Take a moment to look over the example that we have below and see if you are able to spot where the problem may be with this part of the code:

```
Def __init__(self, name, age):
    If isinstance(str, name):
    Self.name = name
    Else:
        Raise Type Error("Must be a string")
    If isinstance(int, age):
    Self.age = age
    Else:
    Raise TypeError("Must be an int")
```

This method is one way that you are able to enforce the type checking if you want to use it, but this can become a mess if you start to add in some more arguments. There is a little easier way to get this done. Using the type_check(type, val) function, you can do the same thing as well. This part would need to be called before your assignment with the __init__ method, but then how would we be able to implement this particular checking when we want to place the attribute value set somewhere else? Some programmers will go to the Java method of setters and getters, but this does not work all that well when you work inside Python.

At some point, you may be interested in creating some kind of program that can add in an attribute to just one of the routines, rather than all of them, and then you want to turn the file around and ensure it is a read-only file. There are a few different methods that you are able to choose with this one, but they are all a bit cumbersome to use.

This is where the idea of the descriptors can come into play and will be useful. They are designed to help you work on any kind of program you are customizing so that you can have a chance to access the attributes of that object. You can use this for many options, including for log access, and even to reuse parts of the code, as you need them in your program.

This brings us to the point of how the descriptors can be used to help with all of this. The solution to some of the issues where descriptors are going to be super useful is to just add it in. the descriptor in Python is an object that is going to be the representation of the attribute value. What this means is that if the account object named the attribute, then the descriptor is going to be an object that is going to hold onto the value of the attribute. A descriptor is going to have the ability to be any of the objects that show up in your code, as long as you implement them with the methods of __get__, __set__, and __delete__.

If you are using an object that is in need of the special method known as __get__, then it is going to be known as a non-data descriptor. What this means to the code is that these objects, in particular, are going to only be read after they are through with the initialization. But one that is going to work with both the

___get___ and the ___set___ method will be called the data descriptors, which

means that you get to take the attribute and write on it.

This may be a bit hard to understand when you get started, but we have some

code to help you learn how these descriptors work and what they are able to do.

We are going to take a look at some of the solutions that came with the issues we

talked about earlier. This will help you to type checking implementation easier to

work with. The code that you would use to help a decorator implement type

checking would be like the syntax below:

```
Class TypedProperty(object):
        Def__init__(self, name, type, default=None):
                Self.name = "_" + name
        Self.type = type
        Self.default = default if default else type()
Def__get__(self, instance, cls):
        Return getarttr(instance, self.name, self.default)
Def__set__(self, instance, value):
        If not isinstance(value, selt.type):
        Raise Type Error("Must b a %*% self.type)
        Sestattr(instance, self.name, value)
Def__delete__(self, instance):
        Raise AttributeError("Cannot delete this attribute")
```

```
Class Foo(object(

    Name = TypedProperty("name', str)

    Num = TypedProperty("um", int, 42)


>>acct = Foo()

>>>acct.name = "obit"

>>>acct.num = 1234

>>>print acct.num

1234

>>>print acct.name

Obi

# attempting to assign a string to a number does not work

>>>acct.num = '1234'

Type Error: This must be a <type "int">
```

Once you have a chance to add all of the code above into your compiler, it is time to break it up a little bit. This may seem like a lot in the beginning, but we will look it over and go through it by steps to figure out what is happening, and how the descriptor was able to come in and help make the code work the way that you want.

What we ended up doing in the code above was to implement the descriptor that we called TypedProperty. This is going to be the class that is used to enforce the type checking on any of the attributes that you want within this code, as long as you make sure that all of the processes happen inside the represented class. Be aware of this that the descriptor is going to happen outside of the instance level, and only inside of your class level.

Now we need to explore a bit about the class instance. When we work to get to the attribute and access it, you will need to use the method known as __get__() for the descriptor. The first argument at this point to bring up for the method will be that the attribute is represented by the descriptor references. Then we move on to the __set__ method so that the descriptor is able to call that up the moment the attribute is given an assignment.

We are getting ahead of ourselves with this, and to help us get a better understanding of what all is happening with the code, and to understand why the descriptor is used to represent the attribute, you have to understand how Python is able to carry out the process that resolves your attributes. Any time that you are working with a type of object in this scenario, we are going to use object.__getattribute__() to help us get the compiler to provide us with the resolutions. This needs to be added into the code to ensure this happens.

From this point, we are going to move on to look at how the resolution comes and how we can use it as part of the precedence chain. This chain is used to ensure we are looking for the right attributes inside of the code, rather than just looking around and hoping we find something, but maybe getting it wrong. The chain is important here because at this point in the code, it is going to provide you with the descriptors that tie back to the data provided, which will show up (in this example) in the dict class, and these will have a priority over the instance variables.

While we are on the variables and which ones are getting priority and so on, keep in mind that the variables are going to have some precedence when it comes to any of the non-data descriptors, and you will find them assigned over the getattr(), which is actually going to be the last thing that the code puts out, because it has the lowest priority out of the group.

Working with descriptors can make a big difference in the kind of code that you are trying to write. It may be possible to write some code that is a bit more straightforward and easier to work with without this. However, as your coding starts to advance and you work with it more and add in some more complexity to it, you will find that there are many times when a descriptor, like the one in this chapter, will be able to come into play and help you to get your code up and running.

Chapter 16: What If Something Goes Wrong with My Coding? How to Fix Common Coding Problems for Beginners

In this guidebook, we have spent a lot of time exploring all of the different topics that come with writing your own codes in Python. We looked at why this is such a popular type of coding language to work with, why you may want to work with this coding language over some of the others, and even some of the steps that you need to take to make sure this coding language is going to work well on your system, no matter which one you go with.

Once some of the basics were out of the way, we explored all of the different parts that can show up in the code. We looked at the basics of coding, how to work with inheritances, generators, loops, conditional statements, exception handling and more. All of these are excellent to learn how to do if you want to start writing some of your own programs in Python.

With that said and done, it is time to move on to troubleshooting your program if something is not working the way that you would like. In an ideal world, you will be able to work on the code and nothing will ever go wrong. However, there are times when your code will not act the way that you want it to. Moreover, as a beginner, this can be really frustrating.

Often the fix for why your program is not working or why you are getting some kind of error message or something else showing up is pretty simple. And it is unlikely that you will want to call someone over to fix simple errors, but you do not want to be stuck either. Even as a beginner though, you are able to learn some of the basic troubleshooting work that will ensure that you can take care of most of the problems that appear in your program, so you can get back to work and create some awesome code. Let us take a glimpse at some of the best troubleshooting tricks and tips that you can follow if your code is not working the way that you want it to work.

Even after small changes, run the code again

The more times that you are able to run your code and check for mistakes, the better you will be. This may seem a bit tedious, but isn't it much better to find an error message after four lines of code, rather than finding it after 1,000 lines of code? Which one would you rather go back and double-check to make sure that nothing is wrong?

You do not want to get into the habit of sitting down with a blank Python file and then spend a few hours coding, without actually trying out any of the code that you are writing. You will just make all of the work that you are doing so much harder for yourself, and when there are a ton of errors that start to show up on your screen, it is confusing to know where to start. It can take forever to go through all of this and fix the issue that is going wrong, and you will probably be ready to give up long before you get anywhere near done.

Instead of putting yourself through that entire headache, consider every few minutes going through and running an update, as well as testing the code out to see how well it works. This way, when one of the messages about an error shows up in the code, you are able to easily pinpoint where the issue is going to be in the code, rather than having to check a ton of it. There is no such thing as testing the code too often, so go crazy with this because it really does make your life easier overall.

Always remember that the more lines of code you decide to write out before doing another test, the more potential errors can come in, and the more time it takes you to go through all of the code and figure it out. Doing the testing more often will make it easier for you to catch the errors and eliminate them quickly. Plus, you will find that doing all of these tests will ensure that you get even more feedback and can learn even more about the coding that you are doing.

Print as many things as you can

As you take a look through your code, you need to be able to look at each line and know ahead of time what values are associated back to each variable. This should be something that is easy for you to do if you wrote out your code in the proper manner. If you look through the code, and you see a value that does not go to a variable or a variable that does not have a value, it is time to stop what you are doing and print out that part of the code. Then, when it is time for you to go through and run the program, you will look back over at the console and see how the values will change, or if these end up turning into a null value in a way that you were not expecting to happen.

There are many times where you will need to print out many different things. You may find that at times you will need to try to print a fixed string before you print out a variable. This will ensure that none of your print statements will end up running together, and then you will have a better idea of where these are going to be printed from.

This can be as simple as complicated as you would like to make it, but basically, any time that you want to check the code, or you want to just make sure that things are working right, and even when things don't look right to you, then it is time to do a print. You can print out something like "print got here" and see whether the code is working well or if there is some kind of mistake in the code that you need to fix.

Actually read through some of the error messages

You will quickly find that many of your error messages are accurate and will actually be pretty descriptive for you. The language runtime tried to execute the program, but it ran into a problem. This would mean that you skipped a step, you had a typo, or something else is missing from your code.

There may be times when you do not understand the message that comes up with an error, but it does try to tell you what went wrong with the code. At a minimum, there will be information on a line number the error is on and you can head to that part of the code and look for where the bug might be located.

It is tempting to see an error message that shows up on the code that you are working on, and not even read it. However, there is a lot of information that you are able to find in the error message, and at least having that information is going to help someone else who comes in and tries to make this easier on you. Taking just a few seconds to read through the error message to see what information you are able to glean from it can make your life easier.

See if a Google search on the error can help

Going back to the idea of the error messages from before, remember that you may not know what all of these error messages are about along the way. It is possible that you see that error message and just sees a block of random letters and numbers that are supposed to go together, and you are not sure what it all means. This is hard to figure out, but there are a few options that are available for you to try out to solve the problem.

Instead of staring at the message in confusion with no idea of what to do next, you can copy and then paste the last line of the stacktract into Google or another search engine and see what comes out. It is very possible that someone else has done some code and received that same error message along the way as well. In addition, they will have asked that question or posted the results of it online somewhere. You can use these answers to help you figure out the next steps to take and how to fix the error.

Depending on the error message that you get, and whether it is pretty specific or generic, you may not be capable to employ this method. It is easier if you can discover it online and get some answers that way. However, there are some situations where this just is not going to happen. This is when you need to just start reading through the code and figure out what the error message is all about and how to fix the problem.

Guess and check

This method may take a bit longer for you to get done, but it could help you out if some of the other methods we talk about just do not seem to be doing the trick. If you try a few of the other methods that we talk about in this chapter, and you still are not able to fix the mistake that is showing up, it is time to do a bit of guessing and checking to see what happens and whether or not this clears up the error that you are getting. Remember that we already talked about the importance of running your code as often as you can, at least after every little section, and this will give you quick feedback to work on.

If you keep up with this, you should have a good idea which part of the code is causing the error. If the error was not there before but shows up after you do a few lines of code, you know that the error is in that new piece of code, and it limits down how much searching that you have to do. You can guess that area and check to see what errors you made.

Now, you do need to be careful with what you are doing here. There can be the possibility in some cases that the fix you try to make will bring in a completely new error to the mixture, and sometimes it is hard to tell whether you are making things more difficult, or if you are actually getting closer to the solution that you want to work with. Try to just make little fixes and see if that helps, rather than doing too much at once and making the situation worse.

Trying out a few options and choices here is going to be important because it will help you to get to the solution faster, while making sure that you really learn about the Python code, without having to ask someone else for help. You will be surprised at how much you are able to learn about coding when you have to troubleshoot your own errors, and you will get better at the coding in the long term by doing this.

Comment out on the code and see if that helps

Every type of coding language that you will work on is going to have the comment, which is basically a way that you can leave a note in your code, without the compiler going through and trying to execute these notes as part of the program. This is advantageous to you because you can choose to comment out of a code that you do not want to run right now, but which you do not want to lose track of. You just need to put the # in front of that line that you want to comment out of.

If your script is long, you can comment on some parts of the code that are not related to the changes that you want to work on. This can sometimes make it run faster and it can make it easier to search through the rest of the code to help find that mistake. You need to be careful when doing this though because it will not help you to comment out of parts that set the variables that the program needs to use later on. If you do this, then you are going to have issues getting the code to run.

When you are done testing out the code and you have gotten it all organized and ready to go, you must go back through and remove these comment characters. This helps you to turn the whole program back on so you can see if it works the right way.

Take a break from the code any time that it is needed

It is easy to really get into the code that you are writing, and you do not want to walk away and leave it. This is a great thing to have so much passion for the code that you are working with. However, if you are looking through all of the details for a long period of time, and the mistakes are not getting fixed and nothing seems to be working out the way that you want, then this can get even more frustrating.

When you get to this point, it is time to take a break. It is easy to want to keep working on the code and hope that it is going to get better for you. However, honestly, this is where your wheels are going to get stuck, and it is likely that you will just make the problem worse, while really bringing your frustration levels up to an all-time high.

Yes, you want to stick around and figure out the code and get it to work out for you. However, you are just going to get more and more lost and ruin the code. Taking a break and getting away from the code can make all of the difference. Whether it is just for a few hours or you take a few days off from the code that you are writing, you will find that giving your mind a break to recharge and try again later can make all of the difference in the world.

Working on coding in Python is intended to be simple and can aid you to write some powerful codes that work well. However, this does not mean there will not be times when you are working on some code and it just will not work the way that you want it to. Following some of the tips above and learning how to correct your own work along the way is going to make a difference and will ensure that you can correct some of the issues that show up in your code all on your own.

Conclusion

Thank you for making it through to the end of *Python Programming*, let us hope it was informative and able to provide you with all of the tools you need to achieve your goals whatever they may be.

The next step is to start seeing what you can do to make some of your own programs with the Python code. There is a lot to learn how to do with this somewhat coding, and hopefully, you have already downloaded the Python program, and all of its folders, and had a chance to work on some of the different codes that we discussed to gain some familiarity with how it works. This can give you a great start to working in Python, even if you have never done any coding in the past.

Many people are scared to get into the process of coding. They assume that they need to have a lot of experience to make this happen, or technical knowledge behind them to see the results. However, in reality, whether you have a lot of coding and computer experience, or you are brand new and just starting out, the Python code is going to be the right place to get started.

When you are ready to learn some of the basics that come with the Python language, and how you are able to use it to your advantage to create some of your own codes, even as a beginner, make sure to take a look at this guidebook to help you get started.

Finally, if you found this book useful in any way, a review on Amazon is always appreciated!

CPSIA information can be obtained
at www.ICGtesting.com
Printed in the USA
LVHW060907120223
739295LV00011B/380